the UNRAVELING

the
UNRAVELING

the price of silence

MEREDITH KELLER

Columbus, Ohio

The Unraveling: The Price of Silence

Published by Gatekeeper Press
2167 Stringtown Rd, Suite 109
Columbus, OH 43123-2989
www.GatekeeperPress.com

The cover design, interior formatting, typesetting, and editorial work for
this book are entirely the product of the author. Gatekeeper Press did not
participate in and is not responsible for any aspect of these elements.

Library of Congress Control Number: 2020949184

ISBN (hardcover): 9781662905445
ISBN (paperback): 9781662905452
eISBN: 9781662905469

This book is dedicated to my granddaughters.
Read and remember the price I and so many others
had to pay when reproductive rights were denied to women.

Silence is the Enemy
of Change

‹‹‹‹

Sexual assault, harassment, rape, and intimidation; all have
shadowed and haunted women for decades. Where was
the outrage in the past? Why were so many women silenced?

When author Jon Krakauer tackled the issue of campus
rape in his book *Missoula*[1], he looked for factors that deter
women of campus rape from telling their stories. He analyzed
rape and the justice system, and he revealed that about one
in five American women have been raped in their lifetimes.
Where were their stories? Buried in shame, layered under
decades of angst.

Similar factors kept a lid on sexual harassment in the
workplace. These were highlighted only after the high-profile
expose of entertainment mogul Harvey Weinstein. The book
that followed, *She Said*[2], documents not only the degradation
women endured but the machine of complicity surrounding
sexual assault by powerful men. Women around the country
were finally empowered to come forward and talk about their
debilitating experiences of harassment with a flood of "me
too" stories. What took so long for public discourse while so
many women suffered in silence, women with wrenching
stories of shame and lost dignity?

The Unraveling puts a spotlight on a period in our history
when single unmarried women with unintended pregnancies
were forced into hiding. From the end of WWII until the

passage of Roe v. Wade in 1973, unmarried pregnant women and their families faced shame and insufferable choices. The alternatives were dismal.

One solution was to visit abortionists—who in many cases were not even doctors—who blindfolded women to protect their identities while the procedure was performed. In 1962, sixteen hundred women, forced into illegal procedures, were admitted to Harlem Hospital Center in New York City for botched or incomplete abortions.[3] Society did not condone abortion and left poor women few choices.

Others had no choice but to take their child to term. They quietly disappeared, spirited away while the scourge of "illegitimacy" hung over them. Societal pressures goaded these pregnant women into exile, to be hidden away with distant relatives or sent to cloistered maternity homes. Shrouded in secrecy, with their identities erased, they were groomed to hand their babies over for adoption and go back into society as though nothing had happened. It left emotional scars.

It was known as The Baby Scoop Era[4], when the dominant societal view was that single unmarried women were unfit mothers. They needed to acknowledge their guilt and shame and give their babies up for adoption. The stigma of illegitimacy forced millions of unwed mothers into maternity homes. It didn't matter if they were valedictorians or working women with two jobs; they were shamed and sent away. Women who kept their babies also faced discrimination as landlords refused to rent to unwed mothers. Social workers warned they would be unable to provide for their babies, and most of these women complied. From 1945 to 1973, it is estimated that four million parents in the United States had children placed for adoption. In the 1960s alone, two million babies were put up for adoption.[5] Women were told to forget them and get on with their lives.

The Unraveling reveals one woman's journey through a period we should never forget, when society dictated what should happen to women with unintended pregnancy. Her feelings of shame and lost dignity began with a single incident on a college campus in 1962 and continued until her secret was finally unraveled, fifty-two years later.

Notes

1. *Missoula: Rape and the Justice System in a College Town by Jon Krakauer 2016*

2. *She Said* by Jodi Kantor and Megan Twohey, 2019

3. Feminist.org, Remembering Life Before Roe

4. *Guttmacher Policy Review*, Volume 6, Issue 1, "Lessons from Before Roe: Will Past be Prologue?" by Rachel Benson Gold, March 2003

5. The Baby Scoop Era.com

Table of Contents

Chapter One

The Unforseen, 2014

———〜〜———

Casually driving onto our vineyard in northern California, with the summer heat burning into the pavement, I am happy to see the full canopy of grapevines protecting grape skins from the searing hot sun.

I'm anticipating a quiet afternoon in my art studio, swirling daubs of paint to capture the wispy fog patterns I see each morning and our brilliant sunsets with evening shadows stretching lazily over the hills above the vineyard.

I get out of the car to check for mail in our rural box. Roosters are crowing, and I hear the clanking sounds of tractors discing the soil in the distance. I smell the musty earth being turned. At the box, I sort through loads of junk mail when my eye rests on a beautifully hand-scripted letter from someone I don't know—someone from Austin, Texas. It's obviously a special card.

Once In the car, I impatiently tear open the envelope while noting the artistic script. Inside were these words: "I hope you find this letter welcome. It contains what I think will be big news. I believe you may be my grandmother!"

This was a seismic shock. Although I am used to tectonic shifts and ground tremors in this part of California, this was a huge jolt to my inner core. Something I had so successfully kept burrowed deep down for fifty-two years was opening up instantly with this letter in my hands. It was like ripping the scab off a nearly healed wound. Ouch.

My body went rigid as thoughts of reliving a shattering story from my past sent waves of shock reverberating through my body. All those feelings of shame were about to boil up again. All would be revealed. I threw the letter down onto the car floor in a moment of panic without reading any further.

Did I want to go down that path? To relive the scenes and open the sores of episodes long buried, all the indignity and chilling details of a story that began on a college campus one night in 1962?

Chapter Two

Flashbacks from a College Campus in 1962

Before I even opened my eyes, disturbing fragments startled me. Random images, troubling images, of a dimly lit stairwell, flickers of light speeding through the night, car lights flashing before me. Then, a dark room and a sliver of light streaming through from under a half-closed door, a shadowy figure hovering over me. These flashbacks were making me squirm. Voices, distant voices, men's voices—was I there? What had happened? Where had I been?

Fear prickled my skin. A sense of foreboding engulfed me. These images from the night before suddenly made me feel as though I had been part of this dark movie.

As the first light of morning broke through the inky night sky out my bedroom window, I sat up in bed and realized I was still in the same clothes from the day before, when I'd stopped by the sorority. Segments of the previous night—of being in a college hangout, the Rathskeller, with friends after finals—came into focus. Then came more of those menacing flashbacks. Was I taken somewhere? Where were those steps leading?

Just a bad dream? Suddenly, my body told a different story. There was a dull ache in my groin. Reaching down I realized

I was sticky, and I caught the lingering scent of fresh sex. My madras skirt was twisted around me. Damn, I thought-this can't be. I threw myself back on the pillow and tried mentally to retrace my steps of the night before. How did this happen?

What had begun as a lighthearted celebration seemed to have turned murky; I could recall only slices of the night: the others waving goodbye, headlights of a car going fast in the night, distant voices, men laughing, a half-closed door. Where were my sorority sisters?

I remembered Pete handing me a drink as he slipped into the seat next to me. It was an odd thing to do—we had not been talking or even making eye contact. Without even a wave from across the room, he just appeared stealthily next to me with a drink I never asked for.

I wondered why he had singled me out. His seemingly aggressive presence set me on edge. I usually kept out of his way. He had a habit in class of scrutinizing people over the top of his glasses. Yet here he was attempting to be playful without really emanating much warmth. Initially intrigued by his move towards me, I soon felt a little annoyed. He didn't start any real conversation but just sat there. Then, he started chanting my name, over and over, rhyming it with *Rathskeller*: "Skeller Keller, Skeller Keller." It felt accusatory as he tilted his head to look right into my eyes. As he held me in his gaze, I wondered, was he sneering or joking? Was this his idea of flirtation? I tried to deflect his jabber by changing the subject.

The atmosphere in the bar was pretty much like that of every other fraternity party on campus in the early sixties: boisterous. Voices rose like the foam on the beer. But this was a weeknight, and even on this large, isolated campus, women had strict curfews. Ours was 9 p.m.; the party would be breaking up soon.

I had always been the quiet observer, never the first to raise my hand in class or spontaneously initiate a social gathering. I was a joiner, wanting to fit in with the latest high school fads, spending hours starching skirts to billow out with my bobby socks and angora sweaters. Growing up in fifties conformity, I never wanted to stand out. Last night was no different. I was not the ringleader but an astute spectator from my corner.

As Pete and I went on talking, mostly about him, he sat there flicking at a foil label while boasting about his summer plans. Maybe, I thought, the real Pete would break through his haughty facade. A bit disturbed by his new attention, I looked away, scanning the room. I saw my sorority sisters stand up; one of them glanced my way and signaled they were ready to go. But at that moment I was glued to my seat, unable to bounce up with them. What was wrong? Why didn't I get up to go as well?

What happened next? Did I go somewhere with Pete? I lay in bed dazed, pieced together what had happened the night before, and felt shame wrapping itself around me like a wet blanket. The increasingly obvious denouement was chilling. Realizing I had apparently been taken somewhere for sex made my body stiffen. I didn't even like Pete. I could not erase the sluggish way I felt, lethargic but not really drunk. And, with that thought, my initial disbelief melded into feelings of detachment. No tears. No screams or tantrums. Realizing I had been sexually violated by someone I barely knew left me numb—chillingly stone cold.

Crawling out of bed, I went to look in the mirror for clues. Pulling down my lower eye lids, I saw that my eyes were clear, not bloodshot. Instead of feeling highly emotional, I felt sort of desensitized. Numb. Baffled and upset that I could not remember details of the night. "You idiot," I scolded my image in the mirror. "Why can't you remember? You're a seasoned senior, not some naive freshman guys pounce on."

My freshman year I'd learned the intentions of men at those Thursday night fraternity socials. In essence they were "meet ups," with guys looking us over as potential dates for their weekend bacchanals. My popular sorority fielded many such invites, and the dating dance began at these socials. Upperclassmen were especially interested in the new crop of freshmen. The nubile co-ed, away from home for the first time, figured as the prime target for poaching. These convivial gatherings gave cover to the real intent, a form of dating service. Senior women learned to be selective. Although not seriously attached to anyone by my senior year, I had known many of these men in the bar that night from fraternity socials and parties over the years. Trying to recreate the scene from last night, I focused first on the familiar faces who'd been in the bar.

The dimpled, ruddy, outdoorsy guy, Robert, I remembered well. One snowy winter night he rounded up a bunch of us to go tobogganing. Not usually the adventurous one, I soon found myself sitting on the tail end of the toboggan and soaring down a snow-packed hill with this rowdy group. Everyone was warmed by a flask of brandy. Then several of us on one toboggan hit a rock, sending me flying into the air and then to the infirmary with a compressed disc. It was a fun-filled night with a bunch of his spirited friends until we hit that rock. Later, it was Robert who drove me to the infirmary and became a real hero-figure for me.

Another beaming baby face at the bar was that of Al, who owned one of the few motorcycles on campus. Everyone knew Al. He was a jovial, good-hearted guy. While I was dating his fraternity brother, Jeff, Al allowed the two of us to borrow his cycle for spins around campus. With my klutzy manner mounting a motorcycle, I blistered my ankle badly on the cycle's hot pipe. That made me lose interest in motorcycling but not Jeff. While we were dating, Al was always the big generous friend just as he seemed last night.

The night wasn't making sense. These were my buddies. What had gone so wrong?

I glanced around my bedroom. It sure didn't look like any sexual encounter had taken place here. Nothing was out of order. That was the problem with this room. It was too starchy and prim, with chintz pillows and matching curtains, like a bedroom straight out the pages of *Good Housekeeping*. This room was meant to look proper. It reflected the way I was raised in the fifties, properly. But here the wallpaper was fading, and to me the room reflected a tedious middle-class life, layered with domesticity just like the layers of wallpaper pasted on over the years. I hated this room and the reason I was here this semester.

In my first days as an unworldly freshman on Penn State's campus, I had realized that that the nucleus of social life centered around "the Greeks." The campus was isolated from urban centers or diversions, so the fraternities set the social stage. My first semester, my resident assistant had recruited me into her sorority. Carol was a bubbly campus leader with big dimples and exuded personal warmth. The same was true within her sorority. Their hand-squeezes, serenades, and promises of companionship reeled me in. They didn't disappoint. I was soon firmly in the fold of Greek life. While the fraternity men lived in gracious stone mansions, the sororities were cloistered in dorms with their own special suite of rooms. These were days of fraternity candlelight serenades and all forms of social Greek rituals. These were all conforming activities that took place long before campus sit-ins and protests. We didn't question authority or policies or much of anything in those days. Compliance to rules, not questioning them, was de rigueur. Strong anti-war activism on this campus had not yet arrived.

My last year I was assigned a boring and ridiculous requirement for graduation, to live in the Home Management House. My Home Economics major required eight of us to "manage" this house for a term, performing the tiresome chores of cooking, shopping, and budgeting while carrying a full academic load. My English lit classes stretched my imagination; shopping for this house did not. Developing management skills was important, but why manage a house? My first choice had been to major in hotel administration, but the college advised against it, saying they "could never guarantee placement of a woman in hotel management." So, here I was practicing domestic chores under the banner of home management.

I longed to be back in my room in the sorority, surrounded by familiar scenery and the continuous chatter of friendly voices. There I could better mull over this mess I was in. Instead, I was waking up in this stiff room with reminders of mundane duties. I was just happy it wasn't my turn to get up and make piping-hot breakfast muffins better than any Betty Crocker could make. I hated these tasks and wanted more from college life than these absurde time-consuming activities.

Back at the sorority, I would be able to pry clues of the night before out of Janet and Nancy. Had they noticed anything unusual? Was I acting strangely? I hesitated to call them, though. What could I say that wouldn't just raise more questions?

Remembering saying goodbye as they got up to leave but not recalling exactly what happened next was exasperating.

They knew I would be heading in the opposite direction back to the house, so we'd just waved. No clues here.

My detachment had subsided; suddenly I was in panic mode, desperate to know what had happened after my sorority sisters left the bar last night. Stepping into the steamy shower, I scrubbed away the remaining evidence of sex, whatever it had been, but I still felt dirty and ashamed. I simply had to sort out what had led to a sexual encounter I never saw coming and couldn't remember.

Yesterday, I'd burst out of my last final and headed straight across campus to the sorority suite. Companionship was much needed after such a grueling final. Inside, the girls were in various stages of finals fatigue, curled up on couches in the living room with bloodshot eyes. Ashtrays brimmed over, empty Coke bottles rattled around, papers with handwritten notes were scattered about. I was in a great mood because the final I had just taken could have curtailed graduation, but instead it had gone well.

I searched the halls for my friends, whom I affectionately thought of as *the four swans*: Dorrice, Jan, Nancy, and Mary, one a homecoming queen, one a class officer, each known for her grace and smile. Here they were, stretched out on the floor in nimble poses, holding their fanned-out cards before them, legs tucked under their skirts. "Fourth for bridge?" was bellowed down the halls as a nightly ritual. They were well into spirited bidding wars. Nancy tossed her long blond hair to one side while coyly eyeing her hand and saying, "I will start with four, no trump."

They seemed a bit punchy from late hours of study. Squatting on the floor to join their circle, I heard them gossip about a jam session the weekend before. "Even Sadie, the fraternity housemother, was gyrating on the dance floor. She must have been looped," Dorrice added.

I was also at that party and remembered "The Twist" reverberating from the rafters when the police arrived to quiet us down. It had been a blast. The beer flowing from kegs had puddled all over the polished wood floor, making it so tacky our shoes stuck to it. It was not surprising for the last blast before finals to be a bit excessive. Penn State was a party school, and this was the usual Sunday jam session. I was twisting away with the rest.

Just then we were exhausted from finals, and the stench of overflowing ashtrays filled our nostrils (but no one bothered to clean them). We felt just like those long cylinders of spent ashes but were also eager to celebrate. As we sat around mulling over how to unwind, Dorrice suggested the usual silver-screen experience in town. A movie was one of the few options on our cloistered campus. At another end of finals evening, someone had suggested the arty Ingmar Bergman's *Wild Strawberries*. We had stayed up late, even though wiped out, debating what it all meant.

"So, what is playing downtown tonight?" I asked. Janet rolled her eyes in disapproval. Maybe it was her *American Bandstand* influence from Philly, but she was the lively one on the dance floor and usually liked more active scenes than sitting in a movie theater.

"Hey," Janet said, "maybe we should just go to the Rathskeller. It is the senior thing to do. We should do it. Let's go." So, we gathered ourselves up, threw on our jackets, combed our hair, and primped in the hallway mirror and headed downtown to the Rathskeller.

The worst of the slushy winter was finally behind us— soggy sneakers, wet kneesocks and all—and I was excited to wear one of my new madras wraparound skirts. Madras was the rage. Those hand-dyed fabrics in pastels, woven and finished in Indian villages, made it to our campus in a big new trend. The fabrics would bleed when washed, making them beautifully muted. I stretched my meager budget by sewing my own madras skirts over term break. Buying one skirt at a college shop, I took it apart to make my own pattern. Once home I bought madras from the brightest bolts of fabric I could find to make my own skirts. Finally, I could slip into my new pink-and-purple plaid. Women would never be caught wearing pants or jeans on campus then. We even wore suits and heels to football games. Shorts, tight jeans and skimpy T-shirts would have been scandalous. We were sedate.

On our way downtown, we passed the campus photographer's shop. I couldn't believe it—a misty portrait of me was hanging prominently in the front window on Main Street. I'd been chosen as the portrait of the month.

"Look who's on display," said Dorrice." The photographer had staged an angelic pose using the new soft-focus technique he'd created for all the sorority group composites. "Not bad," said Janet. "Look at that dewy-eyed look." With my eyes tilted slightly upward, my chestnut hair in a flip, no obvious freckles but milky-white bare shoulders showing, he had captured that look of youthful vulnerability. Even my gray eyes were misty to suggest innocence. Such tricks of photography.

On we went to the Rathskeller while looking to relax from jamming for finals. Inside the bar, loud voices shouted over the mellow voices of the Kingston Trio's "Tom Dooley" and "Scotch and Soda." The long mahogany bar had the patina of years of beer stains and was etched with Greek symbols and carved initials, all reminders of happy times spent inside these walls. The mirror behind the bar reflected all the spirited activity taking place.

We saw many familiar faces through a soft haze of cigarette smoke spiraling through the room, mostly fraternity guys and other sorority women we had come to know over the years. Some guys we knew, Al, Tom, and Jim, slouched over the bar, beer mugs in hand. "Look who's here," they commented as we strolled by. We worked our way around the bar, stopping to chitchat with people we knew. It was joyous. Finals were over and we were marking the moment. The noise level was rising, and I was relaxing among campus friends … or so I thought.

Chapter Three

What I Never Saw Coming

———∿∿———

Now I was desperate to sort out the evening. When had I left ... and with whom? The last thing I remembered clearly was the drink Pete brought me as he slipped into the seat beside me.

Was Pete the culprit? Why me? He had been acting strangely, rhyming my name over and over with the name of the tavern, "Skeller Keller, Skeller Keller." The repetitive name-calling was more demeaning than endearing. But it was in keeping with his usual smug manner. I guessed this was an awkward way of trying to warm up to me.

Pete and I had had a few classes together; I'd always found him a bit narcissistic. Not my type.

He showed his swagger in the one class we had together. It was a hands-on meat-cutting class in the College of Hotel Administration. As we carved up sides of beef, we all eventually looked like part of a crime scene, with red blotches all over our white lab coats. Afraid to wrestle a side of beef out of the walk-in refrigerator by myself for fear of being locked in with all those bloody carcasses, I had asked Pete for help. He'd grudgingly held the door open for me. If I ever asked him a question, I would get the answer in a condescending tone: "Now Meredith, this is the way we do it." He was hardly the big-brother type so I quit asking and did my best to ignore him in class. Why would I go anywhere with Pete?

I remembered him sitting there in his crisp starched shirt and pressed khaki pants. His outer appearance was always perfect, and last night was no different. But what *was* different was the playful glint in his otherwise steely-brown eyes when he finally started talking to me. I was surprised at his chattiness after being so smug.

His approach was quintessential Pete—always very self-assured and outgoing, taking charge of any situation. Using his hands to gesture as he talked was a charming part of his Italian heritage. Last night he'd seemed to be focusing on me exclusively rather than hanging with his buddies. I sensed I was his priority.

Still, with Pete you felt he was always playing a game or a role. What was his game last night?

"So, what are you doing after graduation?" I'd asked, knowing full well that he was stepping into his family business and that he would love to talk about himself and the business he was inheriting. He didn't disappoint. Most of the other guys in his major were heading off to junior training programs with hotel chains, but not Pete. His future was secure, and he exuded confidence.

"You know," I told him, "I could have been in hotel administration, too, but the university told me, 'No hotel will hire a female administrator, so we won't be able to place you.'" This amused him, but he kept swirling his beer and chanting my name in a little singsong, "Skeller Keller, Skeller Keller," over and over. Was he even listening?

When Janet and Nancy gestured they were ready to leave, instead of bouncing up to go, too, I had felt weighed down by a heavy feeling. I waved them on. They knew I wasn't going back with them anyhow, so I sat there glued to my seat, listening through the fog of smoke circling the room and the escalating background chatter. I hadn't had that much to drink. Why did I feel so sluggish?

I remembered feeling cozy surrounded by familiar faces. In that setting I felt bonded and sheltered by our shared experiences over the years. These were my people, men and women I had gradually gotten to know over four years on campus. This was the ultimate social inclusion—my comfort zone. I wondered: Did Pete try to come on to me while I was sitting there? I didn't think so. He was all about himself. Did I stay longer as the act of a rebellious senior who hated curfews? Maybe.

Those curfews bugged me. Waiting tables at the Jersey shore in summer, we'd had no curfews, no monitoring of our behavior or parties. It was a great boot camp, where we learned when drinks were too strong, when guys were too forward, and how to dodge trouble. We had been on our own and it was hard to return to those blasted curfews.

Summers at the shore, I learned all about foreboding situations. When our chef orchestrated a party for the wait staff, I went along for the adventure. Hopping in a cab, we sped through the darkened neighborhoods of Atlantic City looking for a party. As familiar landmarks disappeared, I began to get nervous. We ended up at a bar down a dark alley, foreshadowing trouble. Inside, the drinks were obviously high octane; I nursed mine.

Pretty soon the chef, who I was used to seeing peering over the kitchen counter, winking when I picked up plates, came up to me. That night, his eyes were dancing. He wore a fedora and bright Hawaiian shirt, and he flirted with me while smoking a fat cigar and blowing the smoke into my face.

Impulsively, I snatched his cigar from his lips and dunked it into his drink. I could tell from the look on his face, his eyes bulging, that it was time for me to make my exit.

My Southern roommates, with their "y'all" drawl, didn't sense any danger. They were having fun, oblivious to my encounter. Plotting my escape, I looked through the front door and saw that there were no taxis or even lights down that dark alley.

I stepped outside and scanned that creepy dark passage for a street with any signs of traffic. Instead, I saw the silhouette of a man in the distance. Holding my breath, I started to walk briskly by the man, who was leaning against a post in the shadows. It was a nerve-racking, protracted walk. Shaking, I finally saw glimmering city lights and passing cars ahead, and soon hailed a cab home. I knew when to leave a party.

Penn State had plenty of alcohol-laced parties. Over my years there I learned all about the temptations of intimacy and alcohol. But, that night in the Rathskeller, among so many friends and familiar faces, I'd felt safe. Yet, after the first few sips of the drink Pete brought me, I felt lethargic. What might have been put in that drink I will never know, but what happened next was fuzzy, very fuzzy.

I did not remember any red flags like those in Atlantic City. In this convivial setting, there were only the flickering lights, the smoke stains spreading up the wall, the friendly clinking of glasses. Lively voices surrounded me. The mirror reflected friends deep in conversation; others walked around with frosty mugs. Looking back on that night, I did not think alcohol was an issue. It was a party atmosphere, but we were not drinking heavily; it was like any other party I had attended over the years, the beer flowing freely. Apparently, I was disarmed about any lurking dangers.

Then something I hadn't remembered before slowly came into focus, a revealing piece of the puzzle. After my friends had left, as I was heading towards the coat rack, a familiar face from the bar, a fraternity guy I knew, pulled me aside and said, "Don't go with him."

In a flashback, the facial features of a more mature guy came into focus. His face was rugged, the image of a guy who had experienced life well beyond a college campus. He was the war vet everyone called "Sarge," who was also at the recent jam session we were gossiping about over bridge. A bit older than the other frat guys, he was notably more sedate. He hadn't acted as carefree and foolhardy as the younger guys on the dance floor the week before. I sensed a more subdued kind of guy.

Normally, this kind of direct warning would have set off alarm bells. Sarge must have been observing Pete from his corner at the bar and sensed something wasn't right. But apparently I was in a fog, unable to heed his advice.

My mind was spinning, searching for answers. Why weren't my usual defenses on high alert? How did I project vulnerability? Why was I suddenly fair game? Did I feel foggy because I was exhausted from finals? Had I had too much to drink? I remember feeling bonded to that bench. Just when and how did I decide to leave? Or did Pete decide for me?

I was conditioned to sense danger even as a teenager. My round teddy-bear dad would shore me up with warnings about my evenings out and slip me money before I headed out the door with a date. He called it emergency money, "If you need to call home." Just as in Atlantic City, I always knew when to head home. My antennae were usually up.

With just a vague memory of getting into a car with Pete, I might have thought he was driving me to the Home

Management House. But the images of flashing headlights down an unfamiliar street, of climbing a dark stairwell, hearing voices, male voices, that seemed to be laughing off in the distance, were telling a different story.

Confused as to where he took me, I deduced it had to be his fraternity house. Most of the guys I knew lived in those rambling old fraternity mansions with Greek letters ornately carved over dramatic foyers. Women would never be allowed access or ever be in a fraternity after hours—certainly never upstairs. But there were voices, laughing voices, in the background. How could he have dared to take me there?

I shivered at the next scene: a dark room with the door shut and a crack of light shining through from the bottom. That crack of light, I remembered feeling, might be the way of getting out of there. I needed to get out. And then there was Pete hovering over me as I was looking for an exit. There was laughing beyond that door. Who was laughing? Why were they laughing, and was it at my expense? I drew another blank.

I could not recall with clarity exactly what happened. Connecting dots and flashbacks, I wove together that I had been sexually assaulted by him, a classmate I barely knew and didn't even like. It rocked my self-esteem with a chilling sense of humiliation.

That was sex without awareness. Anger was now mixing with a toxic amount of shame. I don't remember resisting him or encouraging him. Nothing. How was this my fault? The term "date rape" did not even exist in my day. You might unintentionally have sex with a boyfriend—but not be plucked from a bar for that purpose. I was confused, frightened and in need of answers.

Wanting desperately to reconstruct that night, I saw the half-closed door as ominous. I wondered who else knew about this night. What fraternity brothers were aware of this scene? Was the laughing at Pete for boldly smuggling a woman into his room? I had never been to his fraternity. Who could help me piece this together? My sorority sisters would not have answers, and I would be ashamed to admit I just didn't know what happened after they left. Right now, none of these fragments were making sense.

My suspicion was that something had been put in my drink to make me feel so sluggish. Then I must have been taken to his fraternity up a back stairway. How could that have happened to me?

I wanted to talk it out, but taking this story into the sorority would be embarrassing. Although our bonds were strong, those times were overlaid with strong expectations of conforming behavior. Like birds in migration, flying in synchronized patterns, the sorority was one big flock. Standing outside their formation could mean a call for censure. At a recent chapter meeting, the president, shaking her finger at the group, recited the need for "rules of expected behavior." She claimed a few of the flock had broken curfew. I would not dare bring up my mystery evening without raising eyebrows. "You stayed out after curfew and don't remember what happened? Just fragments? You think you were in a fraternity house?"

Earlier that year, a few sophomores in our group had skillfully covered up a serious alcohol-related auto accident. Several had broken bones, one wound up with a crippling hip injury, but lips were sealed. The rest of us never really knew the truth or details. Huddling in their rooms behind closed doors, the culprits spoke in hushed voices, getting their stories straight. If asked how the accident had happened, they quickly shut the discussion down. I wasn't about to stir the pot with my ambiguous story.

Rejoining my flock for my final term, I realized how much I had missed their giggles, the screeching laughter, the late-night chats. Once back in the fold, I hoped that cloud of the sexual assault would just drift away. It didn't. Instead, the whole tacky incident left me feeling robbed. Like when a burglar sneaks into your private space, taking your personal things, you feel violated. In this case, I was not only violated, but I knew my robber. Yet, I wasn't about to share this violation with my sorority sisters.

Sitting around the suite that spring, we often talked about our new lives yet to come outside these protective halls. Thinking life would be brilliant in a big city like New York, Nancy and Mary longed to experience the Big Apple. Those row houses in Philly were calling to others. "Beacon Hill in Boston might be better." I didn't have a destination choice to make, because I had accepted a dietetic internship in upstate New York. I would be moving to the Northeast, just not with them. My friends of four years would soon be dispersing and flying solo outside the comfort of our group.

Blossoms were bursting open around campus, and spring was in the air, but not for me. The incident festering inside felt like a smudge on my character that I didn't deserve. It wouldn't go away. If you had a painful tooth, once it was extracted the pain would be quickly forgotten. This dull pain wasn't going away.

"Not my fault," I kept thinking. It wasn't casual sex with a boyfriend that went too far. Pete was not a boyfriend, not a date, not even someone I liked very much. Just an acquaintance who had highjacked me for his own pleasure.

The casual no-strings sex of the sexual revolution was yet to come. Free love and all those bare bodies writhing to the music at Woodstock had not yet happened. In 1962, on our campus, behavior was much more sedate. Sex before marriage was frowned upon. It might be practiced, but it was still taboo. Many marriages were rushed, and babies were born way before the nine months were up. Chapel marriages on campus were common. Reputations were smeared and eyebrows raised by premarital sex.

I was haunted by the idea that my sexual assault would be perceived by most to be my fault. Women were always to blame. Remembering the laughing voices from that evening, I wondered who else knew I might have been in Pete's fraternity. That was gut wrenching. The humiliation I felt was mine, but it should have been his. My reputation was at stake, not his. It was distressing. But, what was there to do?

Only Pete could fill in the blanks from that night, but I shuddered at the thought of confronting him. He was not in any of my classes now, and on this large campus our paths would not likely cross. With graduation and new adventures ahead, I tried to turn my thoughts to the future. This incident, as harrowing as it was, could just fade away.

Several weeks later, while I was studying at my desk after dinner, I felt a sudden burst of nausea. Making it to the wastebasket in my room in time, I thought it was just an upset stomach—the flu, or maybe something I had eaten. Then I realized, with growing horror, that this sudden burst of nausea was exactly like my sister's morning sickness. She'd described for me how she felt when she became pregnant: "No forewarning symptoms, just suddenly throwing up." Just like tonight!

As I wiped away the sweat that was now liberally mixed with tears, I slowly realized the cruel truth. I didn't have the flu. I might be pregnant. For a few minutes alone in my room I couldn't move. With my blood pressure constantly low, I was never one to scream or yell, but I was simmering in silence. The thought of pregnancy was devastating. Starting to shiver, I felt the bottom drop out of my future. It felt like shattering glass.

That night, as I tried to fall asleep, it was against the backdrop of my carefree, giggling sorority sisters and the soft, round sounds of Ray Charles singing "I Can't Stop Loving You." Wrapped up in romance and planning future weddings, some were playing romantic recordings that were jarring me. I lay awake, eyes wide open, contemplating my gut-wrenching decisions ahead.

As I fell into sleep, my dreams were woven together with haunting stories of back-alley abortionists. Dreary tales came into focus. Women blindfolded so the doctor would not be identified during illegal abortions. Stories whispered about women using knitting needles, drinking turpentine, or relying on bodily abuse to end their own pregnancies were coming into focus. Many pregnancies, I heard, were followed by infection and even sterilization. I was shivering under my covers. What should I do?

Abortion was strictly illegal. Even though the birth control pill was introduced in 1962, on my campus and in that time, it was not widely accepted as safe. No one I knew was taking the pill or even talking about it. I knew of no campus counseling services and no abortionists. There could have been some, but I was not aware of any. I was bereft of ideas. Where would I turn? I barely slept, haunted by the dismal alternatives.

By morning I began to see Pete as a nasty piece of work. I kept thinking of him dragging me to his fraternity and forcing sex at his will—something none of the men I dated on campus would do. And now, I was left to figure out what to do with the shattering consequences.

Humiliating as it would be, I had to confront him. What a loathsome task. Trudging around campus, I dreamt up various scenarios. I imagined cornering him and saying something like, "Hey, remember that night you took me somewhere from the Rathskeller? Well, I just may be pregnant." This was going to be painful. Confronting him with only my sketchy information of what actually happened would be rough.

After figuring out where his classes might be, I waited until I saw his tall figure leaning against a tree, leg up, smoking a cigarette. There he was with his usual confident air and starched white shirt. My stomach felt gnarled and my palms were sweaty, but I strode up to him with my rehearsed comments in mind.

"Meredith, what are you up to?" he said with his usual smirk.

"I am not great. I have a question for you."

He looked a bit sheepish. I mustered my courage. "That night at the Rathskeller, I know you took me somewhere." No response. "I have little memory of that night, but I do know that you took me somewhere, and now I just might be pregnant. So, what happened?"

Staring at me blankly, and showing no emotion, no surprise, no remorse and with no apologies, his almost-immediate response was, "You know, I can get you some pills for that."

I was stunned. He didn't answer my question. He showed no surprise and offered no words of compassion. His was a routine, matter-of-fact response. With that chilling retort, I went silent. That took the starch out of my sails. There was no fight in me. If he had said, "I'd been drinking and things got a little out of control" there might have been a conversation. Instead, he waited for my response. Such arrogance! His silence was an admission of rape without any guilt. Although I had wanted a private discussion with him, I now wished someone else could have been there to witness his callous response.

He held me in his gaze with a stony stare. My voice froze; I could not find the right words. I turned away in disgust, feeling even deeper despair. If he had expressed some form of compassion instead of that chilling stare it might have eased my pain. Instead, his response was, "I can get you pills for that."

Chapter Four

My Graduation Present

Back in the sorority I slammed the door shut and slumped down on my bed as I tried to sort out what to do. It was about six weeks until graduation. In my silent rage, I wondered where I would turn with this chilling ultimatum.

After those first waves of nausea, I thought about calling my big sis, Judy. She would help untangle this mess. Three years older and married with a toddler, her age and experience could help. Not always the sage, or one to make good decisions with her own life, she was still my closest and most trusted confidante. I remembered the pranks she pulled on me and the power she once had over me. I was always tagging after, but she would ditch me and ride off on her bike to join her friends before I could catch up. She'd better not ditch me now. I needed her.

Growing up, I adored my big sister. When she

was on stage dancing at her first-grade performance, I jumped from my seat and ran up to the stage, trying to mimic her moves. The audience was laughing, but she was not. Seething, she shooed me away, as usual.

She led me on many risky adventures. Scavenging through the woods one day, she lifted a big boulder to see the grubs and worms and let it fall, smashing my six-year-old barefoot toe. She carried me home, my tears streaming. When I had to get stitches, she was truly repentant and in awe of my bravery. Because I didn't squeal on her, I gained her respect. After that she accepted me as an accomplice. I was finally allowed into her gang.

We spent our childhood climbing trees and roaming the neighborhood together. She was the fearless leader. During the polio epidemic of 1950, we were confined to the limits of our front yard. We hung out in the trees, decorating ourselves in skirts of leaves like Tarzan and Jane. We had an incredibly carefree childhood. Judy was the initiator, and I was her sidekick. She was the spark plug as I tagged after her, sucking in her endless energy.

We shared everything—not only a bedroom, but all our secrets. Judy was my guide, my touchstone, then and throughout my whole life. Just now, though, I knew her life was turning in the wrong direction. But I still needed her help.

The only phone was in the hall of the sorority suite, where everyone would be able to hear me. I waited until no one would be hovering around to wait for their boyfriends' good night calls.

As I dialed, the clink of the coins echoing down the hall, and I thought about Judy's happier days as the pretty blonde with super-charged self-determination, selling the most Girl

Scout cookies in school, always clamoring to be best. She was the shining star of hope in the family ... but that was changing.

Dee, who always called her boyfriend Johnny to say good night, shuffled out into the hall and stared impatiently. She wanted me to hurry up with my call. I didn't have enough change to keep making long distance calls and stammered, "I'll only be a few minutes longer."

Why wasn't she answering? This was nerve-racking. I needed to talk to her now.

Even though I wasn't as motivated to be a high achiever as Judy, I somehow felt secure, without a driving need to always prove myself. As I bounced down the halls in high school in saddle shoes and bobby socks, my academics were good enough for college, and I was more content with an active social life than an academic one. She was the stellar student.

With all that potential, Judy had abruptly left college. Her education was derailed. Dropping out to marry such a loser, whose main passion was playing bridge, just didn't seem fair. Her life now was off to a rocky start, and it now appeared mine might be as well. I was concerned about her as I placed the call.

When I heard her voice at the other end, my body relaxed. I cupped my hand over the receiver. "I need to tell you something, but you can't tell Mother. I'm in deep trouble." Slowly I started to unravel my story. I whispered about the night in the tavern, a few of the fragments and unknowns ... and then feeling the first signs of what might be pregnancy.

"Oh, don't panic," she said. "You might just be nervous about what happened. It could be a false alarm. Getting pregnant from one night only isn't likely." Her certainty was soothing, but I wasn't so sure.

Hanging up, I yelled down the hall to Dee, "OK. The phone is free."

Maybe Judy didn't want to take on my uncertainties as well as her own. Her life was heading into chaos, with a new child and an irresponsible husband. With her marriage failing, the tedious side of life was getting to her. Her husband grudgingly struggled to make ends meet by selling baby strollers door to door. She never complained and clammed up about how difficult her life had become, but there were clues. In spite of that, I was hoping she would come through and help me out of this mess. She'd always been there to get me out of scrapes … and pregnancy was a big one.

I meandered around campus with the "pregnancy" cloud floating over me. Anger was simmering inside, but I was not one to scream and shout. Thoughts of what those fraternity brothers of Pete's might know about that night were haunting me as well. Did they know it was me Pete had dragged upstairs? I didn't see Sarge on campus, but I would have averted his eyes even if I did. Worse than my hurt pride was the realization that my graduation plans might be in jeopardy. Judy had never seen her graduation, leaving after the first two years of college to get married. Mine was within reach, just a few weeks away.

Back in my room, I thought about calling Judy again. I needed some next-step advice. Even though her life was churning with turmoil, she would be more help than my less-worldly mother. My compassionate Mom would just not grasp the complicated story from that night at the Rathskeller. I dialed Judy again.

This time, she was more realistic. "OK. You should be tested by a gynecologist. Come back home and get into Pittsburgh."

She didn't express any urgency. With just a few more weeks of classes before final exams, I decided to wait it out rather than hop a bus to cross the state. I needed to focus on graduating; I would be home soon enough. Besides, this just might be an imagined problem, as she'd originally said.

The last few weeks of classes, I was just going through the motions—dragging myself from one to the other. Trying to study, but easily distracted with worry. I stumbled around campus in a daze deeply disturbed, but I felt I just needed to get through graduation.

At a tennis class one morning Janet said, "Hey, your game is really off. Didn't you have your Wheaties?" Janet was tall and lanky but nimble, and that helped make her a better tennis player. She deserved a better partner than me that morning. I just wasn't up to tennis or sharing any revelations about my condition that morning. As we walked along, I quickly changed the subject.

As the final semester was winding down, it was time for the usual fun "spring week" activities. My head wasn't in any of it. Watching my sorority sisters punching colorful mounds of crepe paper into chicken wire for our float, themed around the musical *South Pacific*, their exuberance was lost on me. Mary with her broad smile and blonde hair swinging was leading them as they gustily sang "There Is Nothing Like a Dame" and "I'm Gonna Wash That Man Right Out of My Hair." I wondered, how could I wash away the memory of Pete's assault and my life-changing dilemma.

I was envious. They were so carefree, so mellow. I was feeling desperate and just buried my inner feelings even deeper.

After graduation I was supposed to be heading to my internship. Now there was this darker unknown. I was just marking time these final few weeks so I could get home to face the consequences.

Meanwhile on campus, the sun had warmed the soil that had been crusted with ice through the winter. It seemed everyone on campus moved outside to study. The scent of freshly mown grass was in the air, and the lawn was blanketed with women in bathing suits spraying water or baby oil on sun-starved bodies to encourage a glow. Sunbathing trumped studying for finals.

I sat with them on the lawn, feeling a bit better warmed by the toasty sun. I was itching to unburden my story. Then, I imagined their reaction if I were to suddenly blurt out, "Guess what? … I think I might be pregnant."

Instead, I just sat there reminiscing about our lighter moments. "Remember Sunday mornings how we would read aloud those *New York Times* nuptials and snicker at the snobby verbiage, "Mr. and Mrs. Eldon Wallingford Snodgrass, III, announce the engagement of their daughter to the nephew of the railroad magnate Filthy McNasty IV." We had perfected just the right snooty inflections.

Marriage wove in and out of our discussions. There was the undercurrent in those days that we were sent to college to find a husband. None in my group were engaged and we were looking forward to big adventures on our own.

"I am really going to miss our late-night talks," I said as they sat dabbing their bodies with baby oil.

"Yeah. Remember how we quizzed Rachel about her relationship with Robbie?"

I asked her, "What if you married Robbie?"

Assimilation was a timely topic, especially for those of us dating at the same Jewish fraternity as Robbie's. "Oh, I know she was nervous about how her family would react. Does anyone know if Robbie ever met her parents?"

Phillip Roth's book *Letting Go* and the movie version that followed hit a chord with us. The plot involved the relationship between the only child of Jewish parents, Paul, and Libby, a Catholic. When they marry, her father cuts off financial support. Roth had a way of bringing social issues of the day right into your face. We massaged Roth's story late into the night.

Letting Go was laced with sexuality, and it was way more explicit than our discussions ever were. It was not our comfort zone to talk about our own sexual experiences. How could I ever bring up that I was sexually assaulted in a fraternity? My own perceived shame kept me quiet.

This might be hard for younger women today to understand but, respectability was the mantra of the times. After World War II, people were so glad to have moved out of the poverty of the Depression into home ownership and a more comfortable middle-class life that they carefully guarded their reputations. In the sorority, as we sipped our first coffees, we often mimicked our quirky mothers' sense of propriety. "What would Ethyl say?" would float through our conversations. Janet's mother Ethyl, from the prestigious Main Line of Philadelphia, was a widow trying to keep up appearances in that upscale part of Philly. She was the mom most often impersonated. A strict schoolteacher, Ethyl managed Janet's life so that she and her sister would be raised "properly and without incident." Ethyl's idiosyncrasies were charmingly outdated. When Janet called to tell her mom she was heading to Fort Lauderdale for spring break (with "Where the Boys Are" blaring in the background), Ethyl had

had fits. "You are going where? You're all staying in one house? Men, too? Who is the chaperone?" This was 1962, just a few short years before the women's liberation movement emerged across campuses.

When graduation day finally came, a bittersweet feeling overcame me as I watched the colorful ribbons flying that bright June day at the cap-and-gown ceremony. I was going to miss them all ... our paths were forking finally. Celebrations were all around me, with the flourishes of the band and flashes from cameras. My parents proudly stood by as I hugged and said goodbye to my dear friends of four years. As we packed up our cars, my eyes teared up as girls called out, "Write me," or "Come to New York City once we get settled."

Possibly pregnant, I was not heading East for my internship as they thought. Biting my quivering lower lip, I still hoped for some sort of miracle to get me out of this predicament.

Saying goodbye was hard. I wondered when or how I would see them again. Some were bound for adventures in the skies. Regardless of their degrees, some signed up as stewardesses, with promised escapades around the world. One art history major was heading to the gallery scene in New York. Several were student teaching in New York. I seemed to be heading into a cavernous unknown.

I was going home to spring painful news on my parents. Behind closed doors I would have to burst their bubble of pride amidst all the homespun celebrating. The balloons would deflate as my embarrassing problem was brought into daylight.

The thought of the unsavory discussion ahead made my stomach flip. These were the two people who meant the most to me, the two I would never want to hurt.

Would they understand the fact that I could only recount flashbacks? I anguished over their "What will the neighbors think?" attitudes in this small town. How would I tell this complicated story—just lay it at their doorstep? I felt I had to come clean at last and tell them that pregnancy just might be my graduation present.

Chapter Five

Disgrace

———∿∿———

My pregnancy would be shocking enough for my parents, but in our small industrial mill town of 25,000 it would be a scandal. Nestled along the Allegheny River near Pittsburgh, mill towns like mine were a mix of people who mostly had to sweat to make a living. They were as strong as their sinewy shoulders. Within our town, each ethnic group created their own tight community, and their solidarity was based on religion, ethnicity, and family. They gathered in their own private halls, lodges, and alliances, and there were many such halls in my town: the Moose, the Elks, the Knights of Columbus, Sons of Italy, the Slovenian Club, and more. These ethnic clubs were not only spirited centers for dancing and drinking, but also for social support and spreading the gossip of the day. Oh, boy!

Religion was the glue in my town. Perched on top of the hills were three large Roman Catholic churches—Irish, Polish, and Italian. There would be a collective gasp in the Irish church when the marriage bans were read on Sunday if an Irish girl was marrying an Italian. You married your own.

Many eyes were watching as we grew up in that city of steeples. Priests in those days were the arbiters of all behavior, especially for teens. From their pulpits, they would chastise high school students for their sins—sins like necking in public. They were also known to inform parents during the homily of the grave misconduct of their teenagers.

Yes, there were always scandals. Beginning in grade school, I had my first inkling of disgrace. When school was out each day, we ran to Mr. Weigel's candy store a half-block away. It wasn't really a store but his home, open up for business in his living room with enticing penny candy counters up front. When we walked in through his screen door, pennies and nickels jangling in our pockets, we saw a showcase full of temptations like Mary Janes, Bazooka bubble gum, jawbreakers, wax lips, Chuckles, licorice twists, and Tootsie Rolls. With all these brightly wrapped confections, our young eyes would glaze over as we agonized over our choices each day.

Suddenly one day, his store simply closed. There was no explanation for our tiny ears, but we overheard parents saying Mr. Weigel had asked one of the little girls to take her pants down. "Pedophile" was not a word second-grader kids knew or understood, but the community did.

Another scandal smacked into me at a tender age of ten when the town's bank president was caught embezzling money. He lived respectably in a bungalow a block up from us. I knew his kids well. His daughter and I were close at the time, and I had a crush on her older brother George, our neighborhood paperboy. He always had teasing words for me, like, "Your shoe is untied, freckles." I thought he was so cool, earning his own money delivering newspapers. A few days after the scandal broke, my friend called me to go over to her house and keep her company. I wasn't sure how this would go. He was going to prison. As I walked up the path, I noticed their window shades were all drawn, making the whole house seem a little foreboding. Suddenly I was nervous and feeling sorry for the whole family. Once inside, I came upon her dad sitting in the kitchen, hunched over a cup of coffee. I was trying hard to find the right words in my ten-year-old vocabulary to say something sympathetic. While pretending nothing was the matter, I just ended up saying "Hi, Mr. S." I found it hard to look him in the eyes.

The gossip surrounding his fall from grace lingered for years. Even sadder, was the fact that their son George caught polio delivering papers in the cold rain and ended up in a wheelchair. Life didn't seem to be fair to me. These were good people, and while their dad was in jail, his wife and kids were paying a heavy price. She had to work, take care of her crippled son and suffer the alienation. Eventually they moved away.

My unwanted pregnancy was sure to set the tongues in town wagging. I would be casting long shadows on my family. Social mores were strongly in place here. Mine was a juicy scandal in the making.

This kind of news would not only be upsetting for my parents but for my younger brother, who, at the highly impressionable age of sixteen, was struggling to define himself among his peers. I didn't know his adolescent demons, but I did know he was a bit awkward socially, and this news would just add to his anxieties. He would be grist for the rumor mill in high school and maybe even be subjected to searing comments. "So, somebody knocked up your sister!" I shuddered at the thought.

My sensitive kid brother had a tough demeanor, but I knew this would be a sore spot for him. Mean jabs from peers would hurt.

But I was concerned mostly for Mom. She was obsessed with what others would think. Growing up in the fifties, I felt that strong drive for social acceptability. Mom got stressed if my dad raised his voice in the house, if her windows weren't spotless, or if the garbage can remained in the driveway too long.

"What will the neighbors think?" became her constant commentary. Respectability wasn't just her issue. It was common to be very concerned about other's perceptions of you in the community.

The collective code of behavior back then was a fear of ostracizing behavior. Oh, boy! Pregnancy and the issue of illegitimacy were hot buttons. As I thought about what I was about to tell her, I imagined the shame spreading over her.

Dad would be an even tougher challenge. I would have to dig deep into myself to muster the courage to face my father and his furies. He was our moral compass, the one ushering us to church every Sunday. We all knew his unspoken expectations of us.

In my day, parents weren't into repeating the reassuring "I love you" every day. In fact, I never heard those words from my dad, ever. I just knew he loved me. He didn't have to tell me. Parents didn't wear their emotions on their sleeves or even share them often. It was "Do as I say, not as I do." You knew what was expected behavior. You just didn't talk about feelings. Like my Germanic dad, you were stoic.

Dad did have a temper, and we all knew when to disappear. When his checkbook didn't balance at the end of the month, he would rage at my mother as we ran for cover. But a pregnancy, impugning our family character, was way more serious.

Under this cloak of conformity, the consequences for me in my hometown could be huge. Everyone knew all about each other's lives—the good, the bad, and all the unsavory secrets. All were eventually revealed and spread. How would my town react?

In some ways, these were the best of times for middle-class America. There were no homeless people on the street, no skyrocketing rents, no college debt. Everyone had jobs. Work was the backbone of the middle class as I knew it. My dad, a blue-collar union electrician working on large construction sites in Pittsburgh, could afford to send his kids to college. We lived next door to the head of the research laboratory for ALCOA. It appeared to be an even playing field.

Our town was an ethnic stew, yet prejudice existed. There were rivalries between the Italians and Irish and even Protestants and Catholics. Dating outside your religion or skin color brought looks of disdain from adults, including mine.

While my generation built bridges with various ethnic groups, our parents' held on to their old preconceived prejudices. When I dared date across the ethnic divide, it would bring comments from my dad like, "Not that Mick!," "Another Wop!," or "That Pollock!"

At our biggest event of the summer of 1954, the annual town picnic ay Kennywood Amusement Park, I embarrassed my parents by boldly walking hand in hand with my handsome Sicilian boyfriend they knew nothing about. Emilio was a dark, good-looking kid from class who even gave me his bracelet to wear in junior high. I knew I was dancing around danger, parental contempt.

My old-maid aunt, while sitting primly on the bench watching the passing parade of people, nudged my mother. "Look at that nice white girl with that dark-skinned boy."

Mother looked up and said, "Oh, my … that's our Meredith!" When I got home I heard all their niggling comments, but it all washed over me. Emilio was a buddy and I didn't care what they thought.

But, in that car on that ride home from graduation, I had the jitters thinking about what they would think about my news. There were so many facets to my complicated story. How would I delicately describe a rape I barely remember? How would they react? I imagined the exact moment when realization would click in. The pain of an impending pregnancy would slowly spread like a stain over this proud family, their smiles disappearing.

My anger at Pete was smoldering under the surface. He had tarnished my reputation, my self-esteem, and my pride in the graduation I had worked so hard to accomplish. Now, I would likely miss my internship in the fall and the continuous thread of friendship with sorority sisters and face a very fuzzy future.

I was momentarily calmed looking out the window at the serenity of those familiar silky, rolling hills of western Pennsylvania. My butterflies subsided. In the front seat, I noticed how Dad was proudly dressed for graduation in a suit and tie, Mom in a cloche hat and gloves. They were proud people, products of a surging middle-class post World War II. With the unprecedented prosperity then, they could afford to send their kids to college to achieve the dream that had been out of their reach.

With a flick of her wrist, Mom dangled a cigarette out the front window, with the nonchalance you might have seen in movies of the day. She turned and said, "You were so agitated, fit to be tied, the first year we drove you up here. You spent days packing and unpacking." I remembered I had worked so hard to earn money for those tweedy skirts and matching sweaters and then fretted the whole way there they might not be right for big-campus life. I could sense in this moment in the car that Mom was very proud I had reached the finish line.

Dad scratched the back of his neck. He wasn't used to wearing a suit and stiff-collared shirt. Loosening his tie, he said, "So where are those sorority friends of yours going next? They seemed like a good bunch." He was a people person and apparently approved of my girlfriends. That was something.

This peaceful moment in the car would soon vaporize.

I debated how to begin my awkward story for them. Something as nasty as sexual assault needed a delicate touch. I kept remembering Dad saying, "Never do anything you would not want to see in the headlines." Or, "You only get out of life what you put into it." How would he accept a sketchy story, with only bits and pieces of an incident I could hardly remember? I was barely able to piece it together myself, and now it had to be told.

Watching mother lighting up yet another cigarette, I shuttered anticipating her response. "What would the neighbors think?" It would unhinge her in ways I could not predict.

Would she see that this was not as simple as "my fault" for being in that bar? Would she understand that drinking is one thing but raping is another? There were other men drinking in the bar, and they did not move to take me out of there for their pleasure. Would she comprehend that someone I wasn't dating or didn't even like that much took advantage of me? Would she be there for me?

She had a track record of going to bat for me when growing up. Could I count on her now? In third grade, when a rather sinister teacher named Miss Steltzer caused me grief, she was right there. I always tested well, and across the aisle was Janie, who was just as adept as me in our weekly spelling tests.

Actually, we eight-year-olds were rather bored with the tests, so had a race to see who could spell the word the faster. Miss Steltzer would walk around the room calling out the word. When Janie and I looked at each other's paper to see who had finished first, she came up behind me and said, "What is this? Cheating?"

I tried to explain our game, but she took out a red pencil and wrote CHEAT boldly across it. She took it and said my test would be hanging on the chalkboard for the PTA open classrooms coming up. Terrified and sick to my stomach, I went home that afternoon and said I needed to go to bed. Mom knew something was up. She dragged what had happened from me piece by piece.

"She did what?"

The next morning Mom was up early. Dressed in hat and gloves, she marched with me to school to have a talk with the principal. I watched in awe as my paper with CHEAT written in red pencil was taken down. I was absolved.

A few months later, Miss Steltzer came into our classroom and made a big show of first closing the door. Then, in a hushed tone, she said, "You are taking an important test today, a standardized state exam." She walked to the chalkboard and proceeded to write out the answers to the test. Of course, the kids went home and told their parents. Miss Steltzer didn't last long in our school system. She was the CHEAT, just projecting her own flaws onto a poor eight-year-old like me. Mom had shown her mettle—if my mom could take on Miss Steltzer, she might be there for me now.

Like most moms of the fifties, she was a devout homemaker. After school our kitchen was always filled with the aroma of sautéed onions or bubbling sauces. Her cooking style was strongly influenced by our Polish butcher. Through his tutelage Butch had taught her to infuse pot roasts with herbs and layer in carrots and onions to caramelize while roasting slowly. Through him she became a rather decent cook.

A visit to Butch was her Saturday morning ritual. He was her link to cooking beyond the recipes of the day that began with a can of Campbell's Cream of Mushroom Soup. Peering over his meat counter and resting on his pudgy arms, Butch would take time to tell her what cuts of meat she could buy, then walk her through just how to prepare them. Pork roasts smothered with sauerkraut, glazed onions, and caraway seeds was a family favorite. With her own mother bedridden, Mom had never learned much about cooking. Butch was a blessing.

All that devotion to homemaking was comforting as a kid but also embarrassing to me as a teenager. Coming home from high school one day, I saw Mom hanging off a ladder outside our house, her hair wrapped in a scarf and tied on top like in the Rosie the Riveter posters of World War II.

Cringing, I shrunk down in the front seat of my boyfriend Dickie's long Buick. His flashy chrome fins, blinding in the sunlight, always caught attention in town. Wilting at the sight of my Mom in that dowdy attire, bucket in hand, Dickie noticed her as well and asked, "Who is that?"

I was mortified. How embarrassing that my mother was washing windows like a charwoman in some old novel. Dickie's family owned the biggest department store in town, and his mom was always smartly dressed. I felt Mom was living a narrow life, and I wanted her to reach for the brass ring—or any ring.

My graduation held that promise of a bigger life for me. But now I saw that bigger life starting to slip away.

On that long ride home, I tried to forget the weight of my burdens by focusing on happy high school years. Memories of the mid-fifties flipped by like the pages in my yearbook.

Jamming into those flashy cars of chrome, we would head down Main Street in groups, especially after football games. Those streets were noisy with the cars circling town, and Georgia and I would be waving wildly to those heading to Sam's, our hamburger hangout. Inside, you had to shout to be heard over the jukebox music of Buddy Holly's "That'll Be the Day" or Chuck Berry's "Johnny B. Goode." Sam's reeked of greasy fries and grilled sliders. It was there that we loudly celebrated our football stars like Bruce, the quarterback and usual hero of the night, who was my very first crush in grade school. In third grade he let me wiggle his loose tooth and wrote our names in chalk on the sidewalk. I always had a huge soft spot for Bruce and those nights at Sam's.

Another memory that made me smile was wearing my boyfriend's class ring around my neck and feeling very connected to him senior year. The two of us spent hours at those steamy drive-in movies where our friends would go car to car with flashlights trying to catch who was necking. When Burt Lancaster was wrapped up with Deborah Kerr in *From Here to Eternity* in that torrid beach scene, the windows would fog up.

No one worried about drugs and alcohol then. Sex was the biggest concern. The birth control pill was not yet an option. Abstinence was the only option. In spite of those evenings spent at drive-ins, or parking wherever we could, we were strongly hemmed in by attitudes and oversight. Parents cared what time you came home, and the porch lights would flicker off and on if you lingered too long in a car. Even though they were, no doubt, aware we were all parking and petting, they were silent about the consequences.

Roused from my trance of happy high school memories, I began thinking about the downside of living as a pregnant, unwed mother in a small town. One could not escape a bad rap here. Like with the flashlights at the drive-ins, there were no secrets here. There were snitches and rumormongers. My best friend Georgia experienced serious scorn at the hand of the town gossips. Character assassination shadowed Georgia from early grade school through high school. Her fault was having an attractive young mother, a divorcee, who dared to entertain single men. That set off the neighborhood whisperers, mainly a set of corporate wives who huddled together over bridge parties, gossiping about Georgia's mom's "trampy" behavior. Of course we kids overheard those diatribes. I remembered hearing one mom say, with a thick Southern drawl, "Why, that woman is nothin' but white trash!"

Gossip cast Georgia in her mother's shadow. Even when we were younger, she wasn't invited to all birthday parties, despite being the prettiest and smartest of us all. Georgia and I were very close growing up, and her mom was super sweet to me. I loved when she would pick us up after school in her convertible with her auburn hair and long scarf flying in the wind. I thought she was a classy lady, but the neighbors did not.

Later in high school Georgia became a bit of a flirt. Maybe it was her way of trying to be accepted, at least by boys. In any case she was already labeled unfairly.

Poor Georgia suffered this unfair bias all through school, snubbed at invites and later by all the high school sororities.

In our yearbook she wrote to me, "You have been a fantastic, bestest friend, quite understanding and fine. If I have never told you this before, I know you understand that things have been very confusing for me."

The saddest part of her story I didn't fully learn until many years later. Her father had sexually abused her at a very young age. She was barely aware of it. Later, in her forties, her mother finally told her, "That was the reason for our divorce, my dear." It was shocking news. Georgia mustered up the courage to tell me this, saying, "I only vaguely remember something seeming a bit odd, but I was very young. I missed my dad terribly with that divorce. When he left, everything changed."

When Georgia was in her early teens, her dad committed suicide. It was very sad. We, including the gossipmongers, never knew the whole story. Town gossips don't comprehend the irreparable damage they can inflict.

Divorced women, though often humiliated, were slowly becoming a known entity then. However, single unmarried mothers didn't exist in this town, or at least we never knew about them. Illegitimate, a term not used today, said it all. How would I and my family be regarded here? What would we be facing?

Chapter Six

Bracing for the Talk

———∿∿———

Which parent to approach first? Although Dad had a soft spot for me, he would be a hard nut to crack. His fury could come out of nowhere. One morning at breakfast he threw a toaster across the counter at my mother—it missed her and bounced onto the floor. I never knew the root of his frustration but still remember the crashing sound breaking the early morning silence, reverberating through the house.

He was a man's man, knowing just which stories to spin and with whom. A raconteur by night, he always had an audience when slipping onto a barstool at his favorite hangout, Chick's, the only stag bar in town. We were not allowed inside, but apparently he was at ease in this setting, where he would buy rounds of beer for his buddies, a mix of town elders and neighbors. I'm guessing they bantered about baseball statistics for the Pittsburgh Pirates, as well local scandals.

The famous mafia family living among us *sotto voce* offered grist for the rumor mill. Even the mayor, who was friends with Dad, looked the other way at the illegal gambling and prostitution under his nose. People in our part of the state knew of our town's reputation and referred to it as "Little Chicago." My hometown was a steaming cauldron of scandals.

To most who knew him, my father was a jolly man, celebrated for his salty sense of humor. How would he deal with my story from his barstool? Knowing how the men at the bar chewed over each other's stories, I wondered if he would dare share the one I was about to tell.

Growing up, dinner with Dad was unpredictable. As we gathered around the dinner table, Judy would carefully calculate his mood before pushing any of his hot buttons. His crisp sense of humor could easily fade when he was annoyed with us. We saw that temper when Judy had tricked him into giving her more lunch money—that didn't go over well when Dad caught on to her scam.

And yet, Judy loved to debate Dad, especially after her civics teacher taught her to question what she read. When the McCarthy hearings began in 1954, Judy was a senior in high school. I remember her locking horns with dad, honing her debating skills and challenging his views.

"You know, Dad, everything you read in the papers isn't always true."

"Those Hollywood screenwriters knew what they were doing. It was subversive," he said.

"No, it wasn't, and they lost their jobs."

"Your teacher is a little too soft on Communism," he snarled. "Just what is he teaching you?"

For reasons I could never comprehend, Judy loved to challenge Dad. I was happy to be the quiet observer of their verbal jousting.

But the one thing Judy could not do was unlock the key to his softer side. I could, and I knew just what strings to pull.

I was more infatuated with Elvis Presley than politics. Strangely, Dad supported me in my obsession, in spite of the fact that Elvis had a renegade bad-boy image similar to James Dean's. I found a blue suede jacket downtown at Sears and enticed Dad downtown to see it. When I tried it on, he said, "What is it you like about this jacket?"

"It's just like the jacket Elvis wore on his album cover."

The price tag drained his color and then his pocketbook. I wore that jacket until it was threadbare. Dad could be soft as putty sometimes. I alone could make Dad crack a smile in the middle of one of his rants by daring to call him "twinkle-toes." He was heavyset and often in bare feet, and I could see a smile beginning to curl on his lips when I said, "There goes twinkle-toes in another rage." Then I knew I had him.

I knew he was a diamond in the rough. As a young man, he was handsome, with slicked-down black hair and soft blue eyes, graduating high school at just fifteen.

"If you graduated high school so early, why didn't you go to college?" I asked one day.

"My Mom died of cancer. I was just twelve. So, your Uncle Deemer and Uncle Harry raised me." He didn't tell me, but I later learned his dad was a useless alcoholic. "My old aunt was a teacher, and she tested me for college entrance. She wanted me to go to night school at Pitt. So, I went by train each night after work. Your mom would wait up for me to bring home hamburgers, for our dinner. We were already married, and I needed to take care of her, too. Then the Depression came, and that was the end of night school for me." Although a college degree was out of Dad's reach, he managed to send each of his three kids to college.

His own fractured family didn't deter him from driving home a sense of morality for us. Even though he displayed forms of racism and bigotry, every Sunday he took us with him to the Episcopal church. Mom dressed us in hats and gloves, but Dad was the driver of our religious upbringing and a respected member of the vestry. Going to church with him was our special time to connect.

One sultry Sunday morning I had invited Georgia to come along with us to church. There were no windows or cooling breezes that day, just the bright sunlight shining through the stained-glass windows, making dancing patterns on the pews. It was hot, humid, and still. Beads of sweat were forming with all the standing and kneeling for the liturgy. Georgia wasn't used to this routine. Women used their programs as fans to try and cool down. It was all a bit much for Georgia, and I heard a loud thud. She had keeled over in a dead faint. Dad scooped her up and took her outside onto the grass.

When she came to, he was kneeling there soothing her, saying "That's OK, Georgia. It was too hot today. Why don't we go get some ice cream?" In spite of his fits of rage, he could be very gentle and very sweet.

Which dad would I face when telling my story? The lion on a raging rant or the pussycat? I wanted to broach the subject with just the right note. Maybe I should try and gain his sympathy right away. But how? His stoic, Germanic black-and-white thinking ways would be hard to navigate. He could deal with facts and logic, but there were so many missing pieces—just flashbacks. One thought was to string together what I knew to make the flashbacks look like facts but, that wouldn't work. The one unmistakable fact was that I was sexually assaulted and just might be pregnant.

I anticipated his questions. "Why did you even get into his car?" he was sure to ask. Yes, I was twenty-one. "Old enough and ugly enough to know better," he would always remind us. "Didn't you have money for a cab?" This was going to be rough. I wasn't taken at gunpoint or with a dagger. Acquaintance rape was not that kind of thing. Would he ever understand that I just couldn't remember what happened?

While I also fretted about how to approach Mom, my guess was that she would be much softer on me. I thrived under her mothering ways but wondered how this simple woman who lived more within our walls than the outside world would react to my sexual assault. I doubted she had ever been in a bar but knew how ominous that would sound to her

Would Mom comprehend that what happened was not my fault?

Would she care about the trusting feelings I'd had being among friends that night in the Rathskeller?

Would she understand my betrayal by a classmate I didn't even like?

"What were you doing in a bar?"

"How much had you been drinking?"

The whole subject of babies and pregnancy would be touchy for Mom. Several miscarriages early in her marriage had wounded her deeply. Her eyes would grow misty, telling us how she had waited ten whole years to have a child who finally lived. There were stories of Dad having to bury a stillborn, and the sadness of that had engulfed him as well. For them, children were sacred. As kids, it made us uncomfortable to hear Mom retelling her stories. We three knew she cherished babies. She would be conflicted about a pregnancy of mine.

It pained me to see how reliant she was on Dad. It was a fifties thing, but she leaned on him for everything and even rejected learning to drive.

"Mom, you could even buy your own cigarettes so Dad won't know how much you are smoking. Why not give it a try?"

"No, I don't need to learn."

She was more content with domesticity. She swaddled us with affection, sewing our clothes and filling the house with the yeasty fragrance of dough proofing and pastry baking. She was content spinning a warm cocoon. That was the normal fifties household. Baking at night was her way of wrapping us in her web. While we were studying on cold winter nights, enticing chocolate aromas would swirl around us as she pulled gooey cookies or brownies from the oven. To Mom, food equaled love, and both were ever present in our home.

Now that I was in trouble, Mom and her domesticity no longer embarrassed me. Maybe she was not sophisticated about the ways of the world, but she was very adept at building a solid foundation for us. Wanting more for her was simply me superimposing my newly formed values on her. She wasn't about to change. I desperately needed her help and was hoping she could handle my news without it cracking the bedrock of her very being.

Once home, I wanted to talk with her privately first. But, since were still celebrating my graduation, I decided to wait until morning, after Dad went to work.

After waking and wandering through the house, I looked for the most comfortable place to talk. Still in pajamas, I curled up in the kitchen and waited for Mom to appear. A pot of Folgers coffee was percolating on the stove. Our house always had that lingering aroma of burnt coffee and cigarette smoke. The scent of Dad's cinnamon-dusted toast from earlier was still lingering in the air.

Our kitchen was Mom's sanctuary, the place she felt most at home. After Dad left for work, I refilled the coffeepot and set it on the stove. Mom had her apron on, ready for the day, when I asked her to please sit down for a minute. Our kitchen table was the scene of warmer conversations between us when I would complain about bruised feelings or tell her about my newest crush.

The house was quiet except for that pinging sound of the coffee perking. I wasn't sure how to start, but knew it was time. Setting a cup of coffee by her and placing her cigarettes nearby, I was ready. She was a chain-smoker and would light one right after the other. We would need a big ashtray.

She lit her cigarette, leaned on her elbow resting her chin on her hand and with wisps of smoke framing her face, said, "OK ... what's the matter?"

Looking first at the floor and then into her soft hazel eyes, I said, "I am in big trouble, Mom. I might be pregnant." She looked dazed, motionless, like a cornered animal. "The hard part is I honestly don't know exactly how it happened. I don't remember it."

"What? How could you not remember?

"A few of us were celebrating the end of finals at the bar I took you and Dad to after graduation. Some guy I barely knew came over to me with a drink and sat with me while my sorority sisters were circulating around. When they were ready to leave, I suddenly felt glued to the seat. I just don't remember what happened after that drink. But, I do know he took me somewhere for sex."

"This scares the bejesus out of me. Why do you think you are pregnant?"

"Because I've had morning bouts of nausea."

There was a thud of silence. I watched her reaction as I plodded on with the story, her already-pale complexion turning alabaster. Her reaction seemed to come in slow motion.

She started shifting in the chair, putting her hand over her eyes, twisting her mouth, lighting even more cigarettes, running her fingers through her thinning hair, pulling on her ear. Finally putting her cigarette down, she started pacing the kitchen.

"Oh my God. What a mess!" she thundered, then: "We need to find a gynecologist fast, and I don't know any. Maybe we need a trip into Pittsburgh." She sat down and composed herself, then added, "Let's not tell your father until we know for sure." She looked away as if still in thought. "Oh, my!"

Chapter Seven

Dilemma

———∿∿———

Mother was at her best when she had a problem to solve, and I had given her a devastating one. We began frantically searching the yellow pages for gynecologists. We narrowed the list, made calls, and managed to get an appointment for the next day.

On our ride into Pittsburgh, the car was thick not only with her cigarette smoke but an abundance of apprehension. I had a bad case of the butterflies. I calmed myself by reminding her of the fun we'd had in the past, shopping in Pittsburgh for prom gowns and fancy dresses.

"Mom, do you remember shopping for my winter coat in junior high, and I fell in love instead with a black velvet fitted one? It was hardly a practical winter coat." I was trying to get her to stop nervously lighting up one cigarette after the other. "I love how we arrived at the stores early. Waiting for the doors to open you treated us to warm sticky buns at Stouffer's. Then, we raced through the three big department stores to narrow the choices. Over lunch you let me plead my case."

"I don't know why I let you talk me into that that fitted velvet coat...but it looked like it was made for you."

Mother was a frugal shopper and did not usually make snap decisions. Over lunch in Horne's Tea Room, we would make a list of the options we had seen. On the back of a napkin or a torn piece of paper, she charted prices along with practicalities. We debated, and often she caved to my first choice. We went home tired but exhilarated.

As we were nearing Pittsburgh, I grew increasingly apprehensive. Even at twenty-one, this was to be my very first gynecological exam.

As we entered the cold, sterile doctor's office, the acrid aroma of alcohol filled my nostrils. Although the gynecologist turned out to be a warm and comforting woman, I shivered just looking at the examining table with all those cold instruments. My first internal exam was awkward and uncomfortable, and my teeth did not stop chattering. When the ordeal was over, I sat up on the edge of the table waiting for her to speak. When she did, she addressed us both.

"Well, you are about twelve weeks pregnant," she announced, confirming news we did not want. When mother heard the words, her body started twitching and pain spread across her softly wrinkled face. My heart broke. She was visibly trying to maintain some composure.

The doctor very softly and sympathetically asked what we intended to do. Mother said this was all sudden news and we had no plan. The doctor talked about group homes for women in the area. Abortion did not seem to be on the table. Although women always found ways to have abortions over the years, it was strictly forbidden and illegal then.

One thing I knew about my mother was her strong sense of justice. She knew that my pregnancy was like a sadistic joke. She said, "Look, I don't want my daughter to feel the shame of being in a group home. She's suffered enough already. Aren't there any other options?" Her voice turned pleading, suffused with anxiety and pain.

"Wait while I make a few phone calls," the doctor said and left the room.

Mother and I looked at each other with puzzled expressions. I was shivering from the frigid exam room, the crisp white sheets, and all the uncertainty surrounding us. Mother was pacing while she lit yet another cigarette. The silence seemed like an eternity.

Mom must have known of the degradation of those maternity homes. Identities were erased, names never used, even the clothes were not their own, as they were barraged with harsh reminders that they were bad women there to learn a lesson and hand their babies over for adoption.

The door finally opened and the doctor said, "Well I may have some good news for you. It's possible for me to arrange for you to stay with a family on the other side of the state. They would take you in and, through a doctor I know there, you will receive care until the birth and then consider adoption." Relief spread through this awkward moment as a resolution seemed to be taking shape. The mood changed as we calmly discussed the details. Now I had a plan to present to my Dad—but I was still dreading that talk.

When just a toddler, Dad would hoist me on his shoulders and take off for the cellar to shovel coal into the furnace. I begged to go down with him every night. It became our own routine. Watching those flickering flames and just being with Dad was our special time together. From then on, I tagged after him whenever he had chores around the house.

His sterner side I learned at age five. Dad kept a few shiny Canadian coins in his dresser. Fascinated by these shiny objects I pocketed them and told my mom I found them on the street. When he heard that he pulled me up on his lap and said, "You know I would be very sad if my little girl ever lied to me. Where did you find these coins?" After a long pause and a few muffled sobs, I came clean. After that, I could never lie to my Dad.

His fun-loving and carefree style was just a smokescreen to his strong Germanic black-and-white outlook on life. There were winners and losers in his world—no shades of gray in his expectations for each of us.

The scene I was about to describe for him was murky, clearly not black or white. It would not hold water for him if I couldn't cite the facts. Instead, I had just flashbacks of a bizarre night that never made sense to me. As his favorite, I was about to deeply disappoint him.

In my house we had never talked openly about sexual behavior or rules of expectation. The closest I came to censure from him was when our porch lights would flicker on and off if he thought I was in a car with a guy too long. The following day it was never discussed. These were just his unspoken rules of behavior.

Later that afternoon Mom let the cat out of the bag to my brother and sister, so I needed to launch into my talk with Dad as soon as he got home. I approached him while he was sitting in his favorite reclining La-Z-Boy, not unlike the one Archie

Bunker sat in in *All in the Family*. The rest of the family quietly disappeared, and I went over to him as he leaned back, shoes off, reading the paper.

Kneeling down, I looked deeply into his soft gray eyes, and said, "Dad, I need to tell you something serious." As he peered over his spectacles and the top of his paper, he reminded me of Doc from *Snow White and the Seven Dwarfs*. Seeing I was troubled, he dropped it into his lap.

"I really don't know how this all happened", I began with tears welling up, "but this is all I can remember about a bad incident at college. After our last final in spring a few of us went to celebrate at the Rathskeller ...," and I went on to cover all the other sketchy details I could recall, looking all the while for any signs of his reaction.

Was he comprehending this, that maybe Pete perceived my vulnerability when my friends left? Was he able to grasp my side of this muddled night?

To my surprise, he showed no recriminations. When I finished my story, he just stared off in the distance, finding it hard to square what I had just said with his image of me. His face turned pale while his eyes narrowed into a fixed stare. No rage, but a stoic, blank look.

His stony reaction filled me with a deep sadness. He then got up and disappeared upstairs. I followed him, only to hear him sobbing in his bedroom. The family heard it from their corners of the house, from wherever they had taken refuge. I had never seen my dad cry, ever. It was painful to witness. When I quietly approached him and sat down beside him, the only words he could muster were, "You are not a toy!"

The shame a father feels when his daughter has been defamed or wronged must be like being punched in the stomach. I have never forgotten those words. "You are not a plaything that is easily discarded." He deeply felt my pain but had no other words.

Feeling his remorse, I tiptoed out of the room and shut the door. That night I heard every minute ticking by, tick, tick, tick. Lying awake, it seemed to echo through my body. For my father, this was especially devastating. The daughter he had tried to protect especially through her teens had been victimized and he felt helpless.

Through his own torturous, sleepless night, Dad was hatching a plan. The next day he went to visit a man he greatly respected, seeking legal advice. This must have been a difficult call for Dad to make. As a devout Episcopalian, vestryman, and head of the Building Committee for our church, Dad was calling on the deacon in our church for help. This man was an esteemed judge in the county known to us as PK. It pained me to think that Dad had to humble himself in front of someone he so respected. PK asked Dad to bring me by so I could tell him the story in person. Another shameful experience to face.

That afternoon, in his den, after much head-shaking PK said to me, "Sorry about this kind of guy, but we have a plan. Can you give me the culprit's name and hometown?"

PK would be contacting him to arrange for us to meet, including both fathers as well. No lawyers would be present, just Pete, me, and the two dads at a motel halfway between our two cities. It was shaping up to be a "high noon" moment.

When that day came, it was a stifling hot, early-summer morning. Suffering from a bad case of nerves coupled with the lingering nausea that accompanies pregnancy, I was a wreck with this juggling act. As I got dressed for the showdown, I wondered if makeup or lipstick even mattered. I was no longer trying to be attractive but to just get beyond this torturous day.

My shoulder-length hair was wet at the neck from perspiration. I looked in the mirror sideways and wondered how my stomach would look as it started to swell. Always priding myself in being fashionable, showing off my figure to its best advantage, now I would be learning how to hide it. The sundress I wore was loose enough to conceal a figure just starting to thicken.

This meeting would be the most humiliating experience yet. I could feel that Dad was agitated about the task ahead and barely spoke on the long drive. Wearing a suit I knew he considered this very serious business, deserving a certain dignity, even if only through appearances.

A feeling of dread seemed to settle over the car. Dad appeared to be deep in thought and was not at all chatty. I was sadder for my dad than for myself. He looked so very uncomfortable.

Watching him out of the corner of my eye, I observed his body language. His demeanor was somber as he gripped the steering wheel tightly. I was thinking the only times I ever saw him wearing a suit were happy occasions. This was not.

When we arrived, this inappropriate setting felt more so when we pulled up to the front entrance. Flashing neon signs suggested "a comfortable cheap stay." Here we were at this chintzy-looking motel where temporary nights were spent, often for casual sex. This wasn't the right place to be deciding my destiny. It all seemed sinister. I was trembling a little as we both ambled towards the entrance. I wondered if bitter words would fly. Would my Dad show hostility. Would he bring up the wrongs done to me? That Pete could not deny himself the pleasure of opportunity?

Pete's father was more gregarious than Dad. He reached out to shake Dad's hand, saying, "Hello, Mr. Keller—and this must be Meredith."

Our eyes averted, Pete and I awkwardly refrained from engaging each other. Then we all walked towards a suite of adjoining rooms. We sat facing each other, and after a few uncomfortable exchanges, my father cleared his throat and nervously commented, "In my day, people in this situation would just get married." I was dumbstruck. Clenching my fists, I thought, how dare he speak for me or suggest a solution like marriage. I was old enough and ugly enough (as he often said to us about making decisions), so why was today any different? I could hardly catch my breath. Dad waited for a response.

I was seething. Did he not understand I had nothing but disdain for Pete?

Losing his poker-faced countenance, Pete's father relaxed a bit, showing a softness I had not yet seen, and slowly agreed by saying, "Well, that's right." Turning to me, one bushy brow slightly raised, he said, "What do you think about that, Meredith?"

I was shocked by this twist, and before I could even form an answer, he added, "Why not go into the other bedroom and think it over. Pete, what would you think?"

Pete just shrugged his shoulders and looked down.

Stunned at this "Think it over" directive, I realized this huge, life-changing decision apparently needed an immediate answer. The clock was ticking. The moment of truth. Decision time. With no sister Judy to pump me now, I was going to be all alone on this one. The weight of the choice that would change my life was unbearable. Marry someone you had no feelings for? Apparently, this would give the parents a sense of respectability. Tick, tick, tick.

Really? How could they consider this? There was no love here. I had no respect for his son, who had never even offered as much as "Sorry." How would anyone want to start a marriage based on rape? What part of my story still wasn't clear to them? But I was not about to start defending myself now. Did these two fathers think that because we were college graduates this might work? Did they think we had been seeing each other? Maybe the marriage idea was offered because their own reputations were in question. Pete's dad owned a successful inn, and his son's reputation was at stake. Never mind my reputation. Both fathers obviously felt the heat of the situation.

Emotionally drained, I sat there staring at the faded wallpaper. Would my life be washed out and worn like this motel room? The attempt at a "shotgun" marriage was upsetting and brought to mind my own parents' quick marriage. Mom thought she was pregnant at seventeen, when in fact she was not, but they ran off to get married anyhow. My Aunt Evie had told me, "They were so much in love, holding hands and calling each other endearing names like 'D' for *darling*." I was shivering just thinking of a life with Pete.

I took a deep breath to center myself. Regaining my composure, I walked confidently back to the room where they were waiting. All eyes were on me. I firmly announced,

"This is a terrible idea. Our situation is not based on anything like love. What kind of a beginning could that possibly be?"

No one responded. I was startled that I had found my voice so easily and forcefully, making my thoughts known with such conviction. Were they serious about a marriage or just following a lawyer's advice? I quietly added, "I am prepared to go it alone."

In Dad's pocket was a legal document to cover expenses during the pregnancy including compensation for the couple caring for me. As he handed it over for signatures, I saw both fathers exhaling and starting to relax. They were relieved the ordeal was over. I felt sick.

As we walked away, I was secretly angry at Dad and slammed the car door a bit too hard. He had never mentioned this "marriage strategy" before, and I wasn't sure if it was on advice from his lawyer or from him. I wondered why I wasn't in the loop on this but could tell from the stern look on his face that I'd better just drop the subject. This agreement seemed to be the conclusion both fathers were expecting. Pete certainly looked relieved. The verdict was in for the unwed mother. The men awkwardly shook hands and walked away. I had been sentenced to do my time.

What took place that afternoon was simply a payoff. A man would walk free, with no additional strings, no responsibilities, and no pain. I was left with the lifelong fragments of a life to weave back together—the life of an unwed mother bearing a child I just might have to give away.

The road ahead involved delivering a baby surrounded by strangers in a distant place—a baby I had no means of supporting. With the question of adoption still in limbo, I wondered about that whole process. "How would they find the right family?" On the other hand, raising an illegitimate child was one tough assignment.

Thoughts of motherhood were tearing at my moral senses. After all, motherhood within marriage was the shibboleth in our society and right now I was facing the dilemma of my life.

Chapter Eight

Exile

———— ᨆᨆ ————

Unnerved by the bleak experience ahead, I was prepping myself for my time in exile. Now almost five months pregnant, I had successfully kept a low profile away from suspicious eyes by wearing oversized shirts when I went into town, hoping not to run into any classmates who'd ask where I had been lately. My excuses were rehearsed. Slowly I was preparing myself to go underground, lose my identity, and hopefully come out of this a whole person. Would I have the strength to carry this out?

I packed up a few novels and family photos. One picture from graduation day showed my sorority sisters lined by their cars waving. When and how would I ever see them again?

Mother came in while I was packing. "Here are a few maternity dresses you'll need." She had gleaned these dreary, baggy dresses from the local thrift shop. They included horrible flowery prints and one huge navy-blue tent dress I thought I would never fit no matter how big I became. I shoved the dresses at the very bottom of my suitcase. The maternity experience would be dreadful for me.

"Mom, what did you say as to why you were buying these in town?"

"Oh, I said they were for a cousin who lives in Ohio."

Before closing the suitcase, I added a few writing materials, although I knew I would be writing to no one. No cameras. No letters to friends. Nothing would be proudly recorded there. I was heading into soulful isolation.

Where was my anger? It was so unjust for me and my family to bear the brunt of Pete's selfish, predatory night. Not the type to throw a tantrum, I felt that crying over this spilled milk, in this case spilled sperm, was not going to help. I had to focus on more positive energy to get me out of this mess. Where would the next ball in my roulette wheel land? I could have a fresh start or have a complicated entanglement with a child to raise, just like my sister. Would I make it through as a whole woman or be bitter? Maybe the whole experience would shatter me?

All I knew about my arrangement was that I was being taken in by a family in the suburbs of Philadelphia to wait out my pregnancy, with adoption in mind.

Traumatic as this next phase would be, I felt grateful that Mother had saved me from the humiliating group home experience. Judy gave me an earful of what these homes were like, and the picture wasn't pretty. She said in these group homes, their real identities were exchanged for fake names and baggy clothes. If they went into town, they were told to wear a wedding band. Some were pregnant by boyfriends; some wanted to marry. Some wanted their babies; some did not. The parents, priests, and social workers made the decisions. Once girls entered these homes, their autonomy disappeared. They were captives.

"You know those homes are mainly run by nuns who scold them for being bad girls. If the father of the child isn't a Catholic, they tell them the babies are going to purgatory. They remind them they were bad girls who've sinned. Don't you remember that secluded, ivy-covered brick building across the river with the high walls we wondered about? Not a school, not a hospital—it was one of those homes."

So it was that unwed mothers, those bad girls, disappeared into these homes, and now, I was disappearing, too. Thankful my mother found me a reprieve from this kind of institutional experience, I would now have dignity surrounding my experience by joining a family.

On the way to Philadelphia, I anticipated this family who would take me into their fold. The adoption option was still on the table. It seemed to me only logical to give a baby a fresh start with two loving parents and a ready-made family. Pete and his father offered no questions or apparent concerns. My own mother, in spite of having waited so long for children herself, never offered her opinion. She never once reminded me of her own anguish in waiting so long for her own babies. The decision was mine alone. It felt like a volcano was about to erupt, one that would either cause utter devastation or flow to safe place. I was hoping for a safe haven for my baby.

Keeping a child, I thought, could be ragged. Society at that time was very unkind to unmarried mothers. I did not deserve this choice. My parents did not deserve this. They had been disgraced enough. Asking them to shelter and raise a child of shame was nothing I would ever suggest.

The night before I left, I sat up for hours talking to Judy, who kept repeating, "Remember, you didn't even like this man. Don't diminish yourself. Just think of it as a physical process you need go through. Do all you can to keep from getting emotionally attached. Don't even think of raising this baby. Look at my life!"

We were sitting in the living room on Mom's prized but uncomfortable cranberry velvet Victorian sofa with rosewood carvings. I think she was trying to re-create a drawing room from the Victorian era instead of a cozy living room. The one piece out of place in this prim room was Dad's reclining chair. That was where we all ran to grab a seat if he wasn't home.

As we sat curled up as best as we could on that sofa, Judy, her feet in my lap, rehashed her workday. "After feeding Lorna, I needed to catch an early bus to the train station and get into Pittsburgh by 8:45. The work is so uninspiring, just filing papers all day. Later, out my window I could see the political rally for JFK forming. I desperately wanted to join the young people, but I had to get home. I can never be late. It isn't fair to Mom. And, I still have piles of laundry and chores."

It pained me to know how changed her life had become in a few short years. Judy, a gorgeous blonde, had been an aspiring student at Chatham, an exclusive college for women in those days. Somehow, she'd managed to slip off her trajectory and her scholarship. It was a puzzle I never solved. An all-A student in high school, editor of the school newspaper, and general overachiever, Judy had not been on a good path in college. I knew this because we still shared a bedroom at home, and I would overhear intimate details of her dating escapades. Even though I was younger, I could see her judgment in men was questionable. Her top priority, instead of her studies, was a guy from Kenyon College.

From the very beginning, he impressed me as an insensitive effete, bragging about being a descendent of Alexander Graham Bell. His pretensions even made Judy uncomfortable. He grew up in Shaker Heights, Ohio, an exclusive suburb where the city planners made sure all houses fit the right codes in color and appearance. Appearance was everything to him and the mother who raised him. Rules of civility were deeply ingrained in him. However, in our family home, his brand of gracious behavior was off-putting. He exuded a sense of superiority that cost him my respect, but apparently not hers at the time.

I saw how Judy, now divorced, was struggling. She worked as a clerk at the Bell Telephone Company in Pittsburgh, one of the few job opportunities for a college dropout. My parents could not afford to send her back to college.

"It is not easy being a single mom. Just go for adoption. Don't look back," she told me. "When the baby is born, please don't even look at it. You will want it."

Her struggles were being imprinted on me as I saw her life descending into uncertainty. I took a long, hard look at adoption—it offered certainty. I wanted more for this child than being dragged into an unpredictable life. I felt relieved with my decision and was now on a steady course and just needed courage.

A month earlier, my parents gathered their resources and rented a summer cottage, near enough that Dad could still drive to work but far enough away from our hometown. They did their best to keep me close, out of sight of nosy neighbors. Being at the cottage felt a lot like summer camp. My younger brother and I gleefully packed up the car with board games, badminton rackets, and books as we set off for the woods. Judy was going to join us when she could get away.

The fact that the cottage was in a thickly wooded area added to the secretive adventure. It felt like our family vacations like when we used to pack up for life at the Jersey shore, but now we were in hiding.

In this clandestine setting, Mom could relax. We were hidden away from prying eyes. She was at her best with a captive audience and was hovering over us baking pies from fresh wild blackberries and juicy peaches. We brought with us a bushel of super ripe Grand Havens from our back yard, and the two of us decided to see how many double-crusted pies we could make from the peaches, hunting through the kitchen for every possible pie plate or tin.

It was the best therapy. In the kitchen, I relaxed enough to enjoy Mom and her homemaking skills. "You never taught me to roll pastry," I said. So, we rolled up our sleeves, flour dusting our faces, knee deep in peach peelings, and kept at it until every peach was used, and the cottage was filled with the scent of ripe peaches, mixed with almond and cinnamon. The aroma of the sugars and peach juices bubbling over were as fragrant as rich caramels. What had started as a challenge to see how many pies we cold possibly make became a beautiful bonding for Mom and me. Even during college, we didn't spend that kind of time together.

Finally, when that summer drew to a close, Mom and Dad drove me across the state to meet my surrogate family, who lived in a quiet bedroom community outside of Philadelphia. When we arrived, I was happy to see a small, homy Colonial house and an elderly couple waiting to meet us. Alice and Frank, shuffling along with their gray heads bobbing, were like the grandparents I never had. I sensed life would be experienced at a much slower pace.

As I said goodbye to Mom and Dad, I threw my arms around them in gratitude. It had been a beautiful summer of support. Never once had I heard invectives like, "Such a shame!" I was thankful those comments were off the table. Instead of criticizing me, they had bolstered me with love and respect to get me through my final ordeal ahead. I would miss having Mom with me for the birth, but they had done their best. Their hugs were longer and stronger than ever. I was also grateful there were no histrionics when they left me at this new doorstep.

Alice and Frank's home felt cozy and comfortable with crocheted doilies draped over chair arms, typical of elderly retired couples. I saw that Alice kept her fingers flying with crocheting, but not so much in the kitchen. Opening the cupboards, I saw the larder was pretty basic. No chicken broth, olive oil or different kinds of rice, but plenty of Campbell's soup and boxes of macaroni and cheese. I could tell Alice was not the cook Mom was and thought I could help out.

My bright light was the energy emanating from their daughter Marion. She and her lawyer husband and four young children lived on the property adjacent to Frank and Alice. They had an enticing above-ground swimming pool that kept their kids engaged. I immediately liked Marion. She was perky and close to me in age. I liked her sassy style, mocking people and joking lightheartedly. An active mom, she was busy sorting out the slings and arrows of her very active brood. She knew my doctor, Andy, who was her doctor as well. "There isn't a part of me Dr. Andy hasn't seen," she said, winking. She was a bit fresh and I bonded with her, and most especially her seven-year-old, Frankie.

While we drove along, running errands one day, I decided to clarify for Marion my story of the assault. I had no clue what the family knew and didn't know about why I was pregnant. A younger woman like Marion would understand. I wanted her of all people there to comprehend a campus assault. I carefully explained about being in the Rathskeller after finals, when this guy I barely knew had taken me to his fraternity for his pleasure. "I didn't remember going there and didn't know exactly what took place that night." She listened attentively while I walked her through the whole Rathskeller scene and what I vaguely remembered of that night.

Maybe her mind was on Frankie who was acting up in the back seat, throwing paper planes around the car, but she asked only a few questions. She finally asked, "Was Pete your boyfriend?"

I was flabbergasted. Didn't she understand the assault narrative? "No, Marion, he was just an acquaintance who I never even dated but who took me somewhere for sex."

She listened quietly, but we had to get out of the car and the conversation ended there. She picked it up again the next day, saying, "Did you like Pete?"

I was crushed. She apparently didn't believe me. To her, I was just another girl in trouble. What more could I say? I should've raised my voice in indignation, saying, "No, Marion, this was someone I barely knew who drugged me and raped me." But I felt deflated. It was always perceived as somehow the woman's fault. Even among women of the day.

"Don't you want to keep your baby?" she asked me out of the blue one other day.

That was a value judgment I hadn't expected.

"Any new boyfriend would think highly of you if you kept it," Marion added.

Her comments were especially jarring because I did not want ambivalence shadowing me now. I was on my final lap of a painful journey. I wanted my life to be unburdened and to get back on track as soon as possible. I was not ready to be confused when I knew from my sister's experiences that once men found out my attractive sister had a child, they never called back.

I was beginning to feel I was on my own entirely now. No one here seemed to believe that this was a child of rape and that I was in survival mode. He was not a boyfriend. This was not a love baby. I was going to have to build a shield around myself from now on.

The community where Alice and Frank lived was an old, historic one and the seat of a small religious sect. The Swedenborg Church seemed to be a well-organized group with a deep Christian faith. Everyone I met—Marion's friends, the doctor, etc.—were all Swedenborgian, and most I met had gone to the same religious school. This was the hub of their sect, so their lives were very intertwined. Marion and her whole family seemed quite involved. It didn't feel like the diversity I'd experienced at home.

I wondered if some of the other pregnant women I saw in Dr. Andy's office were also women in trouble sent there to wait out pregnancy. It occurred to me that the questions about Pete Marion asked might be used to help Dr. Andy place my child for adoption. I had no clue how that selection process went.

Afraid to ever be seen with my bulging belly in the part of the state where my friends lived, I became a bit of a hermit. To chase away anxieties, I decided to keep busy, very busy. I had never learned to knit but hemstitching was something I could do with my hands. I decided to find a fabric store and bought yards of linen to make elegant hemstitched table napkins.

Carefully cutting the linen into squares, I spent hours pulling threads to make that decorative classic border. While the sticky heat of early Fall poured into that small house, I was upstairs with a fan whirring on the floor with my fingers flying. Stitching was my therapy. Trying not to think of my friends freewheeling lives taking off or my missed internship, I focused on the present, one day at a time, alone, just pulling threads. A stitch in time, indeed. I was in self-imposed lockdown.

Gentle kicks, however, were reminding me of the life inside. This helpless new soul was gently tugging at me. My feelings about giving it away were complex enough without this daily reminder. To protect myself from ambivalence I tried to think of myself as Judy had advised—as just an incubator.

Most importantly, I wanted to deliver a healthy baby. Getting rounder by the day, I snacked on tons of yogurt, the new health food, and took long walks.

Still, no one discussed the adoption. The whole birth and adoption process was a mystery, so I felt I was just treading water while waiting for birthing to begin.

The scent of fall was in the air. The drying leaves tickled my nose with nostalgia. Fall was when I went back to campus, to the football games, to the sorority, all while anticipating new chapters in my college life. All around me today, the foliage was exploding in showy bursts of color. The leaves crackled underfoot. Longing to soak up all that fall splendor, I asked Frankie, the seven-year-old grandson across the way, to be my walking buddy. He was a freckled little guy who came to sit in my lap, like a puppy waiting to be petted. I was tutoring him in math, and we would take walks, gathering bunches of fall leaves, thistles, and berry branches for the dining table. In my heart I knew I would love to have a Frankie of my own someday.

I almost lost it when on our walk one day, he looked up at me and sweetly asked, "Meredith, what are you going to name your baby?" This precious little guy was looking up earnestly for an answer, so simple to a little one.

"I don't know, Frankie; do you have any suggestions?" This, too, the naming of the baby, I had pushed out of my mind. It was a survival technique. Don't linger here and dwell too long in a painful place. Judy's reminders to not get emotional actually kept me centered.

Back in their house, I was beginning to enjoy Alice and Frank's comforting but quiet routine of listening to long-playing opera records before dinner. They mixed a cocktail, usually a Manhattan, and popped a record on the turntable. Opera was a wonderful diversion for me. The arias were dramatic, and I learned over the next weeks to love the pathos of the famous arias from *La Bohème*, *Turandot*, *La Traviata*, and others. For me it was a whole new dimension of learning to feel such drama from the classic opera stories.

As I neared the finish line, I was filled with trepidation and just wanted this final phase to be over. Whenever my parents called, I detected the strain in their voices as well.

I knew Mom had experienced the anguish of delivering two stillborn babies and guessed my delivery would be rough on her. I wasn't wrong. She had been drinking one night and had fallen down the stairs and broken her arm. Though no one, thankfully, told me, I instinctively knew she would be suffering right along with me every step of the way.

After each phone call from her, I would hang up and retreat into my own reveries of a happy childhood. This was my therapy. I would close my eyes and drift back to happy days that formed my early life.

Rather than think about my uncertain future, I went into my past for comfort. Even though I was born in stressful times, just as we entered World War II, those early memories were sweet. I would reminisce about the simple pleasures growing up in our small bungalow. The scent of fresh laundry lingered on Mom's skin and in her hair as she snuggled us at night. Our sheets reminded me of the sunshine we felt on our skin as we ran free outdoors. Would my child experience the same

carefree pleasures? Not under the present circumstances. Not without two parents in a nurturing home.

At age four I was Mom's sidekick as she washed our clothes in a sudsy machine and wrung them out by hand before cranking them through two rollers. That was the fun part, watching shirts flatten out like boards as she cranked away. Then, she lowered the clothesline to my height so I could help hang them with my very own clothes pins. I really would like to be that kind of mom someday. Just not now.

Searing air-raid sirens would wake Judy and me from sleep. When we heard those piercing sounds and saw my parents pulling down the shades for blackouts, we thought it was game time, unaware that our town was a lookout post for spotting enemy aircraft.

Food shortages brought a certain drama into the household. When the ration booklets for food and gas were pulled out of a drawer, there was a big commotion. Clipping coupons, mother did her best to plan meals around the available meats like liver and kidneys. With the shortage of sugar and butter, there were no sweets or desserts, but, we didn't know the difference.

Mostly, I remembered how Judy and I would fight to punch the gel cap inside plastic packets of colorless margarine. Then we would knead it through the package and pretend it looked like butter. It tasted nothing like butter.

Without the luxury of milk, butter, and cream during the war, it's no wonder I vividly remembered the taste of my first ice cream cone. Once the war ended Dad took me to a small ice cream store and I watched them scoop a generous mound of thick cream onto my first five-cent cone. It was a hot day and the cream started dripping down my arms. Licking furiously, I learned quickly to keep it from becoming a sticky mess. The taste was so magical that if I shut my eyes I can still remember that velvety rich vanilla cream. It tasted just like the seeds in the vanilla bean pod I came to know. That day the taste of vanilla as a flavor was imprinted on my five-year-old memory forever.

After the war, when Mom had more available supplies, she turned to her one passion besides homemaking, oil painting. She would cover the dining table and floor with sheets and set up her easel. "Don't bother me today. I am painting and I need you out of the way." As she painted winter scenes from a book of French Impressionists, I was in awe how many colors you could paint into white snow. She tried to interest me in her joy of art by setting me up with dark leaded pencils and kneadable erasers to draw while she painted. But, I wanted to be outside roller skating instead. I had no interest in drawing, but when she mixed up swirls of color for her canvas, I was mesmerized.

In the evenings, Judy and I spent hours lolling on the living room floor around the radio. We would strain our ears to catch the slithering sounds, frightening crashes, or ethereal music that let our imagination fill in the story. Programs like

The Adventures of The Thin Man held us in suspense. Out of that radio console came scary sounds of screeching doors, glass shattering, slowly dripping water, all effects that had us giggling or quaking at the eerie sounds.

Just remembering those radio days, I was missing Judy terribly. Sharing a bedroom for so many years with beds pushed together and our pillows almost touching, we would talk late into the night. I knew all her moods and ambitions and always looked up to her for advice. What would she be telling me tonight? Most likely to remember that I was going through a physical experience only and to not attach sentiment. "Think of it as purely a physical thing you need to go through."

While I waited out my pregnancy, I fell asleep many nights remembering the carefree times, times with no consequences. Revisiting these childhood memories was not only soothing me but giving me the sense of stability I would need for the cataclysm ahead.

Chapter Nine

A December Chill

—∿∿—

"The decision whether or not to bear a child is central to a woman's life, to her well-being and dignity. It is a decision she should make for herself. When the government controls that decision for her, she is being treated as less than a fully adult human responsible for her own choices."

—*Ruth Bader Ginsburg*

Now cumbersome and uncomfortable, I desperately wished the whole ordeal could soon be over. It was Thanksgiving, and Alice and Frank and their extended family were gathering for the feast at Marion's. I dressed in the giant navy-blue maternity dress—the only one that fit now—hoping I would not be too uncomfortable. Feeling awkward as I walked in, my eyes focused on the dining table in their historic stone house. It was set to match their traditional Colonial setting. Tall tapers were lighted with a cornucopia of fall fruits and nuts spilling from the center of the table.

When Mom and Dad called earlier, they detected I was nervous. Judy got on the phone to say, "Don't worry; it will all be over soon."

In any case, I was about to experience motherhood on my own, away from my family. This beautiful moment I had always heard about was about here. I steeled myself.

Before we sat down for Thanksgiving, all in the room lifted their glasses and sang a toast to me that was so emotionally moving I had to stifle tears. That gesture made me feel honored. I was accepted into their fold. Missing my own family that day, I felt very much a part of theirs at that moment.

But beneath my smile, I sat there silently wondering about next steps and how I was to get through this final phase. No one had talked me through the adoption and the delivery date was very close now.

Just a few days after Thanksgiving, the dull aches began. It was a long, protracted labor. Alice called Dr. Andy, and I was taken to a holding room near the hospital—maybe it was a room in his office. I don't remember since I was focused on the beginning contractions. As the labor dragged on for hours, Alice and Marion each came in, taking turns rubbing my back. Women just seem to know how to help each other through those swells of pain. Knowing neither my sister nor mother would be there in time, they stepped up to keep me calm. I was grateful.

Marion wiped my forehead and said the soothing words only a woman with four children would know how to deliver. Grateful for her presence, I squeezed her hand. I was more than anxious; I was shaking.

Dr. Andy, whom I had met several times before, had a warm bedside manner—just what I needed. He put his hand on mine, and the jitters subsided. This man, probably in his late thirties with his glasses raised over his forehead, looked directly into my eyes and talked very gently through the waves of pain that seemed to go on forever. The discomfort continued for so many hours he decided to ease the pain with a mild sedative.

Apparently, I rambled in my subconscious state for quite a while. When I came to, Dr. Andy was by my side. "You were really ranting. Do you remember talking with me? You don't? Listen carefully. You need to know this. It takes very little to sedate you. You were in another world. Always remember that. OK?"

That comment made me connect right away to the night of the rape. "It takes very little to sedate you."

Whatever I had talked about in my ramblings that afternoon, I will never know. What might I have revealed? Many years later, I heard that Dr. Andy, who delivered hundreds of babies, never forgot me and that conversation. Apparently, he confided to a close friend, he knew I had been raped and deeply felt my trauma of that night.

After a few more hours of labor, the final searing pains kicked in. Not knowing exactly what to expect from the actual birth, I was anticipating this amazing experience. That drama denied, I was too anesthetized to remember any of it. Dr. Andy came to tell me later that I had finally delivered a healthy baby girl. I was in a such a deep fog of anesthesia that the pain and the memories of the moment were blocked. Blocked also was the joy of seeing a squirming wet newborn and hearing the first cry. Dr. Andy later told me it was normal to not really feel the birthing process in that drug-induced state. It was normal for those times. Exhausted, I was glad it was over and faded away into a deep sleep.

In the morning, I woke up in a spare hospital room with gray walls trying hard to forget my throbbing breasts and growing maternal feelings. Hearing the sweet sound of babies crying in the distance didn't help. I closed my heavy eyes. To survive this, I would have to focus on getting out of here and going home. Thankfully, Judy was on her way. The only solution I saw was to make a clean getaway as soon as possible.

Judy's words kept echoing in my head. "Remember not to look at the baby. You will want to keep it."

Outside, my dark mood was amplified by the bleak weather, trees bending with icy branches and frigid temperatures diving below zero. It was December first, and my own birthday was tomorrow. How would I ever forget that our two birthdays were just one day apart?

Looking in a mirror, I saw my reddened eyes and realized I was in a state of emotional and physical exhaustion. Giving birth was supposed to be the most joyous moment for a woman. Alone in that room I was steeling myself to deny all that joy.

I was determined not to look at my baby, telling the nurses, "Don't bring me the baby, please." Instead that morning I sat there starring at the blank wall.

Maybe they thought I was in postpartum depression, but they obeyed. Looking back, the nurses were not very nurturing or sympathetic. I sensed their cool reserve.

When Alice came into my room, she asked how I was, then kindly said, "Don't you want to see your baby?" She knew I had given instructions to the contrary. With conflicting emotions, I was overruled by a burning curiosity and a hormonal storm. When Alice left, I then asked the nurses to bring her to me.

Turning down the blanket, I saw dark, curly hair framing a sweet pink face with eyes still closed, that I tried to prod open. When they finally opened, I saw she really didn't look like me or the baby pictures of myself, but radiated her own sweetness and innocence. The hormones that bring new mothers the tingling, swelling breasts, the urge to nurse, and a strong mothering instinct were cascading through my body. I could feel the shift kicking in and tried to suppress them to protect myself. I had to numb myself to the storm of feelings.

How could I deny my own child? The heartache of that moment was scorching. It was being painfully etched in my heart for years to come, knowing I would never know this being I just brought into the world. Looking into those innocent eyes was bittersweet, and the worst was yet ahead.

Alone in the hospital room with no balloons, flowers, or family, I was awaiting the final act in a long, drawn-out drama. The moment I had dreaded was becoming a reality.

Sitting up in bed, still in a mind-numbing haze, I began to think about finally going home. But they soon brought me a bunch of official papers to sign and reality set in. First came the birth certificate. I had to name the father. I stared at the wall, wrestling with revealing his name and giving him that honor or checking *father unknown*. He didn't deserve to be named, but I didn't want the records to show "father unknown." In the end I decided to release Pete's full name. He probably would not wish that, but it was right for the baby to know that her father was "known." There would be *no strings attached* for him, but his name would be forever on the document.

Then, I proudly chose my own middle name as her first name. I have no clue what papers I signed regarding the adoption and never remember receiving a copy. No one broached the subject that I had six months to change my mind. If they did, it was not registering with me.

When Judy arrived, she folded me into her arms. Softly she comforted me with, "Don't worry, the worst is over." Our tears flowed. She had been my savior. Her words had gotten me through this ordeal. The warmth in her big hug said it all.

Later she crept into the nursery to take a peek. "I looked at the baby, and she doesn't look like you at all." Maybe she was helping me to move on and get me into a "flight" mode. We were planning to leave as soon as possible to drive home at last. We were plotting, as we had as kids, the great escape. No one had yet mentioned exactly what was about to take place.

The next morning, I learned that for the adoption to be legal, I would have to personally hand over the baby. No one had explained that before. This would be devastating! How would this happen?

I was told by the nurses I would soon be handing the baby over—to her new parents, I assumed. That morning I was once again alone the hospital room, but by now I was getting used to handling crises by myself.

A wheelchair was brought into my room, pushed by a very officious nurse. You knew right away not to mess with her. When she spoke, she was stern and deliberate.

"Put on this coat—it's freezing out there. We will need to push you down a ramp and into the parking lot."

It was a frosty gray December morning and the winds were bending the trees outside. The nurse helped me on with the coat and wrapped it awkwardly over the hospital gown. All this seemed to happen in slow motion. Few words were spoken. Only the hospital staff were around, and the mood seemed somber. There were no lighthearted laughs or early-morning chatter. I started trembling, and not from the cold. Strangely, neither Judy nor Alice nor Marion appeared when the moment came for me to give my baby away. No one was there to support me. I asked Judy about it years later.

"Nobody informed us," she said. Didn't anyone think that the act might be traumatic for me? Or were they afraid I would change my mind?

The nurse brought in baby Ann swaddled in a pink blanket and gently placed her in my lap. I was afraid to meet Ann's eyes but looked into them one last time before wrapping her up snugly against the below-zero weather outside. The nurse informed me in an almost ceremonial way that we would roll down a long ramp to the parking lot to the waiting parents. The whole process seemed like an eternity. I was shivering with anxiety, and the frost on the windows didn't help. When we were ready, I pulled up the blanket to cover her face from the bitter cold before the long descent.

No one can imagine the gravity and deep sadness of the moment you give away your own child. Even though I had steeled myself well for her birth, the very act of handing Ann over caused a quake deep in my soul. It was an act of severance between mother and child. But I was trying to be optimistic. This would be a wonderful new beginning for Ann. I had hoped that the two strangers waiting at the bottom of the ramp were her new, loving parents. But when I was wheeled up to them, they merely nodded. In fact they were not the adoptive parents but legal representatives. The tears were flowing freely now. When I pulled the blanket back and kissed her goodbye, it was beyond sadness. It was crushing my soul. The waiting woman picked up Ann, and I watched as she turned to leave with the new bundle. As the wheelchair returned up the ramp, I felt my heart thumping. A sharp pain stabbed at me. That

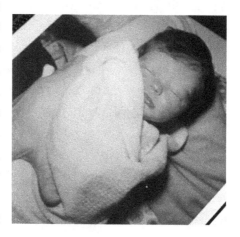

was the most sorrowful moment of my life. Even though I can recall it with crystal clarity, mostly I keep it sealed away, compartmentalized, forever afraid to revisit that sad moment.

Back in the hospital room, I was desperate for Judy to come and rescue me. When she finally walked into my room, she hugged me hard then, in a very sprightly manner, said, "Ready to go home?" Emotionally spent, without an ounce of energy left, I was more than ready to leave this sad scene.

Outside it was the kind of December day when the air feels like knives at your throat. It was too sharp to breathe without a scarf over your mouth. My body was sore from the delivery, my clothes were hanging on me, yet Judy shuttled me into her waiting car. With blankets and pillows piled high for our long journey across the state, we were on yet another adventure together.

I had almost forgotten that it was my birthday, but Judy hadn't. In the car, she surprised me with a cupcake. "Happy birthday. We'll light twenty-two candles when we get home."

Soon I would be home to lick my wounds and assure Mother I was okay. On the long drive home, I shared the whole birth and adoption ordeal with Judy, slowly pouring out the painful details. After listening she said, "Pete didn't have to suffer these deep emotions. He just walked away. No scarring for him. You were left with the pain."

There were many other women like me in those times who also relinquished their babies and never again talked about it openly. It was never mentioned in their families. They just went on like nothing had happened. But, deep down all the numbing shame and pain and sadness was still sealed inside.

My emotions were raw and entangled. The shame of leaving a child behind, the beauty of a new life emerging from my body, the sorrow for what I had put my family through, the resentment and anger at Pete were all knotted together. Quietly, at home, I would process what had just happened. I felt my only way forward was to quit treading water, stay in survival mode, and start swimming back into life.

Chapter Ten

Twists of Fate

I felt that life is like a kaleidoscope. With each twist, new patterns are at your fingertips. Shards of color tumble to striking designs that make you smile or the chips can move into a dull pattern void of any vibrancy. But, when life suddenly takes you to a shattering place and you see the jagged fragments, just keep shifting, shaking and twisting.

Survival during that whole ordeal meant traveling a labyrinth of uncertainty. Spending months being displaced, then processing what had happened and seeking emotional stamina, I just wanted to move on as quickly as possible. I needed to bury all these haunting memories.

I was a changed person. No longer soft on the inside, I was less trusting, more guarded. Fully exposed to the harshness of what life could deal, my outer shell was getting thicker. My inner self was skeptical, realistic, and badly bruised, but also resilient. At least my emotional stamina was intact. I was ready to shape a new destiny.

At home, the family wrapped me in their warmth. We went on to celebrate Christmas together as if nothing had happened. My brother looked at me with sympathetic eyes that wondered what I had been through, but he never asked. Nobody did. This was a closed chapter in all our lives.

My wise mom intuitively knew how to bolster my frayed ego by enticing me into the kitchen to bake. Soon teasing aromas of dense, dark chocolate baking filled our whole house. To this day when I am troubled or disappointed, I just head to my kitchen and pop something chocolate in the oven. It seems to soothe my troubles away. Mom was not one to probe at feelings, asking how I was coping, but side by side in the kitchen we bonded over baking again. I boasted how I had learned from my creative food classes how to not rely on recipes. She would suggest, "OK. Roll up your sleeves and bake your own chocolate buttermilk cake." The challenges to remember basic proportions and add a signature touch were all so gratifying. As we worked together, I looked at Mom through new eyes. Instead of criticizing her for leading a small life, I realized she was the one who had thrown me a life preserver.

On returning home, as I entered the door, Dad gave me the warmest bear hug. It was just what I needed. His gruff ways faded into a distant memory. Without my having to explain what I had been through—since no one asked—Dad, too, seemed to just understand. He was softer with me than ever. I felt an embracing acceptance and understanding from them without any real discussion. Over the next few weeks as we set up the Christmas tree, he asked what I thought I would do next. I was more than ready to carve out a new life, but I knew he was happy to have me stay around. He even began suggesting places in Pittsburgh where I could look for work. I didn't want to hurt him, but I didn't want to stay in the area. "You could work at Stouffer's. They have a big food operation now." In reality, I was itching to move on as quickly and as far away as possible to erase the nightmare.

Yearning for a fresh start, I started scanning the classified ads in Pittsburgh papers. I was ready to leave behind that city of legendary smokestacks and rust when I noticed an ad for *Assistant Dietitian, Residence Halls* at the University of Michigan. I nearly jumped out of my seat. My major in college had an emphasis on nutrition with dietetics in mind. It was sure to get me in the door for an interview at least.

Clinching the job in a telephone conference, I felt elated that I could start moving on now. But I silently wondered after I hung up if I was really ready to move to yet another college campus. On the positive side, it was a distinguished university, and I could now begin a career in dietetics. But finding out I would have an apartment in the largest male dorm, of over a thousand men, where I would be working as the residence hall dietitian, seemed like jumping back into the fire.

How would that feel, being surrounded by men, away from the protective fold of other women? I didn't fear men or put them all in the same category as Pete, but I knew my guard would be up.

Though my dad did his best to talk me into staying in Pittsburgh, I was ready to leap into this new experience and move west. It was time. Packing my bags, I headed to Ann Arbor, not knowing a soul.

It was early February and I was bundled up for the winter weather. As I walked around campus, students trudged along bundled up with scarves covering their faces, but I still detected their youthful enthusiasm. They're animated in a new way. What was it? I was breathing in a whole new campus. The posters and notices tacked up on boards in the student union announced political rallies, poetry readings, and gatherings of all kinds. Ann Arbor seemed to have a totally different, much more activist character. Maybe because it was closer to an urban area than my cloistered university had been. I found it exciting to be in a college town again. On this campus there was an intellectual energy and many close to my own age in graduate programs.

There was a spirit on campus I couldn't define. About the time I arrived, Ann Arbor was becoming a locus of political activism. It was a stimulating stage, and I was satisfied I had made the right decision.

Once I found my quad, short for quadrangle, the dorm where I would be living and working, a tall blonde in a starched white uniform came to introduce herself.

"I'm Jane. I live right next door, and we'll be working closely together". She was, in fact, my boss. I was to be her assistant.

"My apartment is just next to yours." It occurred to me that this might be an issue if we didn't get along. "The students are still on winter break, but when they're here, they're a noisy bunch."

I wondered what "noisy bunch" meant. Just loud, or aggressive? Showing me around the residence hall, she talked nonstop and emitted a very cool, businesslike manner.

"From this kitchen we serve a thousand men, morning, noon, and night." Jane was probably six years older than me and radiated efficiency. No one could call me overly methodical. I saw challenges ahead. For me, this was no longer laid-back campus life as a student. I had a job to perform.

My first reaction to Jane was that she was more imperious than warm. She projected early on this was to be a working relationship, not a social one, and I was her assistant. I guess I wasn't in the sorority circle anymore, and I noticed she rarely made eye contact, and kept touching her glasses as she spoke.

It must be a nervous tic. But, as we'd be working together, I needed to get used to her style. I was feeling nervous about how to relate to her. I could pick friends but not bosses. The first lesson I learned in the real world was to study your boss and learn.

She had a crisp style with the workers, too. "Listen up, ladies, we need to keep this salad bar fully stocked." They were mainly older women, commuting from Detroit, who had worked there years before we arrived.

"Give us a break, lady, we need a cigarette break." This street-savvy, wisecracking kitchen crew would be a challenge for me.

Finding ways to accommodate Jane's management expectations while trying to create my own style was tricky at first. She used a schoolteacher approach, giving instructions firmly. When I was on my own with the kitchen employees, they always tested me. One spouted an off-color, coarse joke, and they all roared. They didn't try that with Jane. As the new twenty-two-year-old novice, poised to give them their daily orders, I looked more like a student. I needed to take control. Should I tell them to knock it off, ignore it, laugh—what?

Assessing the woman who told the joke, I noticed her worn-down shoes and straggly hair. She had a kind face but a mischievous glint in her eyes. I said, "Sarah, do you have any kids my age? You do? What are they doing now?" After a bit of conversation, I learned more about her and her life. Then, I added, "By the way, my mom would never tell me that joke."

As I learned more about them, they became more respectful. When they stood there with cigarettes dangling from their mouths, I learned how to keep them in check by joking along while telling them to put out their cigarettes, put on their hairnets, and wash up.

The biggest challenge was learning to coordinate feeding a thousand men from two different floors. On bad-weather days, hundreds more than anticipated would sometimes clamor into the dining hall at the last minute. On sunny days they would disappear just as quickly. Learning to forecast head counts with all kinds of weather and unusual campus activities had me scrambling.

I was in perpetual motion during mealtime, running between the main basement kitchen and kitchens on two floors hoping the unexpected lines of hungry men would not cause a riot. Actually, I internalized a skill I have to this day, learning just how long a small task takes without looking at a clock. It became embedded in me like a computer chip. I can tell time without looking at a clock. This pressure for performance at mealtime was action packed. Learning the ropes, I felt comfortable there even if surrounded by so many men. This new job seemed to be great therapy, pushing the past sad months into the background.

Maybe because I looked like a young coed myself, it was easier to interact with the men in the dining room. And I received a fair amount of teasing. "Miss Keller, look what I found in my spaghetti?" They would bring in worms they claimed to find in the spaghetti to see how I would react. It was all good natured, and the guys were fun to be around. I adjusted easily, focusing on the mealtime rush to feed all those hungry guys.

It was late winter, and snow and ice were thick underfoot as I trudged around campus. It was one of the coldest days Ann Arbor had seen that year. That evening, in the warmth of the dining hall, I looked up to see a Gregory Peck lookalike bending down to meet my eyes. He awkwardly introduced himself. "I'm Jim, one of the RAs in the quad, and you are?"

I had noticed this good-looking man before in the dining hall and wondered who he was. Living in the dorm as well, he'd gone out of his way to meet me. My heart was pounding.

After dinner, happy just to be inside on such a frigid night, I heard a gentle knock on my door. There he was, leaning on my door to shyly ask, "Would you like to brave the blizzard with me and go to the Pretzel Bell for a beer?" He had such intense brown eyes and such a beautiful smile that I forgot all about the cold and said yes on the spot. After I shut the door I pinched myself thinking of my luck to find such an attractive man living right here in my quad. What was his name? Jim?

When he dropped by later, we laughed about how ludicrous it was to set out with such drifting snow. But I bundled up anyhow, and we trudged out to the Pretzel Bell, the famed campus hangout. Never feeling the sting of the cold, I was warmed by the fuzzy feelings of being with this new handsome stranger. That night there wasn't another soul in the place due to the insufferable weather.

I slid into the seat across from him and noticed when he smiled, he often bit his lower lip. He had and a boyish way of cocking his head while looking deep into me with his penetrating eyes. It was electric. I was totally enthralled.

"What brought you to Ann Arbor?" I asked. Sitting back, I listened to his story unfolding in that cozy bar over a pitcher of beer. He was from a very small town north of Chicago where he once taught high school history. I figured out that he was six years older than me. Once finishing law school, he saw himself as an Atticus Finch, a small-town lawyer. He even joked about being paid in bushels of chestnuts. I was under the spell of his captivating smile and devilish good looks. He had the gift of engaging immediately.

This, I thought, would be a great asset for his future as a lawyer.

"Why law? Where did that motivation come from?"

"That's a long story. Getting to this point has been a struggle." Slowly releasing bits and pieces of his past, he said, "My parents divorced when I was young, and my single mom raised me. I put myself through college playing football, taught high school for a while, and ended up working here as an RA to get through law school. Ambition and a lot of hard work," he mused. I liked that.

He launched into his life at a Jesuit university, where he'd played football. A convert to Catholicism, he'd even won a full football scholarship there. I could tell that experience of conversion was a proud juncture for him. It opened doors.

The snow kept piling up that night and so did our stories. We spent hours peeling back the layers of our lives and looking into each other's eyes. It was magical just sitting in this quiet tavern, watching the snow fall with a new man I found so captivating. I was warmed by this whole scene. Eventually, his fingers touched my hand, still cold from the bitter night outside. It seemed so natural. My luck was changing. It was a new twist in my kaleidoscope.

When it was my turn to talk, I was terrified I would reveal too much. So, I carefully wove together a picture of my middle-class family from a small town. "My parents created a laid-back atmosphere for our wide-open adventures and misadventures. We roamed free and had a rich childhood exploring every crevice of our small town away from our parents' prying eyes." I made a point to talk more about my childhood than my more recent college years.

I explained that I'd always been a joiner, first of a high school and then a college sorority. "Just happy to be on a campus again," I told him, while avoiding going anywhere near the senior year "incident" that tortured me and turned me inside out—and that was still just a few months before this moment.

Tonight, I was thrilled to find such a handsome and charming new friend. Jim was exactly what I needed. He was thoughtful and intelligent and had such a beguiling smile. I was entranced. As we walked home throwing snowballs at each other, I felt his playful nature. It was a new beginning. Those light, fluttery feelings inside meant that the dark cloud that had been following me might just float away.

We could not take our eyes off of each other or stop talking for a minute. From that evening on, we were inseparable. Each night after dinner, I waited for his knock on my door. Many evenings we walked hand in hand around campus. But it became harder to just seal the evening with a brief goodnight kiss. He would pull my chin up to meet his lips very sweetly. Probably because he lived in the same building, I saw him often, and we became constant companions. We were slowly falling in love.

Chapter Eleven

A Tangled Love Story

———～～———

Those were delicious times for me. My painful memories drifted into the background. Our attraction was magnetic. Between classes he would leave endearing notes under my door. We spent as much time together as possible before he had to attend his nightly duties as resident assistant and his "group of wily guys," as he called them.

Some nights we gathered with his Notre Dame buddies and their dates over spaghetti dinners in someone's cozy apartment. I loved being around serious-minded grad students, listening as they chewed over meaty subjects of the law while having fun.

"What is rape?" seemed to intrigue them. They joked around, having almost salacious fun defining it in legal terms. "It's penetration," one of them said. I cringed, knowing that rape was far more than that. What an interesting slant I could have added to that discussion. But I would not dare. That was my secret to keep. I didn't want anything to tarnish this shiny, new relationship.

With my hand in his, Jim and I walked the side streets of Ann Arbor every night. As winter turned into spring, we stared into lighted living rooms of houses, scenes of family life playing out inside, and imagined our lives together. He wanted a cozy house with a wraparound porch, much like the ones we were seeing—an Atticus Finch image of meeting people on his porch. I always gazed into the dining rooms. My dream home would have a big cozy kitchen with a fireplace. I was slowly becoming attached to Jim and kept smiling to myself at my good fortune to meet someone so quickly in Ann Arbor. He had captivated me.

Whenever he would introduce me on campus, especially to his Notre Dame friends, he would add rather emphatically, "She's a good woman!" What was that supposed to mean? I did not want to be labeled as anything. I just wanted to be me. What was a "good woman"? How did they interpret that? Living with my trauma and its labels, I was very sensitive to what that term implied. I wasn't a good woman. I had just given away a child.

Our relationship was sensual, but I kept Jim at a distance, something I don't think he understood. We weren't as intimate as we probably should have been. Maybe I was concerned he might notice my stretch marks. It was not so much a fear of sex as a fear of intimacy, a fear of letting go, a fear of discovery.

I noticed his behavior altered a bit around the Notre Dame guys. If we were in a bar, he would often grab the check, saying, "I'll pay," when I knew he barely had money for a movie. He sought their approval, wanting desperately to belong to that group from the wealthy Notre Dame families of Chicago. That was curious, I thought. He seemed confident enough otherwise.

Still puzzled by his "good woman" introductions, I wondered how he would react if he ever knew my secret. We had not had sex, although we were getting close, but his comment raised a red flag. I did not want his "good woman" image of me to be tainted.

Spring term was flying by. We both knew a painful departure was ahead. Jim was heading home to teach summer school, and I was continuing at Ann Arbor with my residence hall job. The launch of the tender love affair that had kept us floating on air was going to be challenged.

Lingering over a goodnight kiss one night, he took my hands and shyly, almost sheepishly, asked in a soft voice if he could meet my parents and talk about getting married. It wasn't as much a strong declaration of "I love you" but more about the next step he wanted us to take. A wave of excitement rolled through me. After my horrendous past year, the idea of settling into a marriage with someone so warm and affectionate seemed like a beautiful dream. I threw my arms around his neck.

He was very solicitous of me on our long walks, once bringing me a small bunch of spring flowers on his way back from class. That very night he whispered, "You know I want you to be the mother of my children." That was a very sweet thought, but later I wondered what it really meant. Was it based on his love for me … or his desire for a family? What if I couldn't have any more kids? We had never talked about children, but I knew it was a huge concern between a Catholic and a Protestant: Which religion would they be? Though I felt my parents would be thrilled their "compromised" daughter had found such a respectable, handsome man, I wondered what they would make of his Catholicism. Jim was not solicitous of my inner thoughts on religion and our marriage.

"The good woman" image kept burrowing into my mind. I was sure if he knew my story, it would ruin his image of me as his good Catholic wife. That continuous reference made me uneasy. But I was not about to reveal myself. I was too raw. It was too soon. Just six months before, I had delivered and abandoned a baby. That shame was imprinted on me along with new feelings about intimacy. Yet, there was no one I felt close enough to in Ann Arbor to share this dilemma.

I wasn't ready to abandon myself to sensual passion. I simply could not. After all I had been through, I was on guard and afraid of consequences. "The incident" was still with me, unshared and under wraps, locked inside where I wanted it to stay. The obvious electricity between us was noted. Friends referred to us the perfect couple.

In contrast to his easygoing social style, I'd noticed a certain rigidity setting in about religion. He never missed his weekly trip to the confessional, no matter where we were, nor violated his "no meat on Friday" rule. I knew he was expecting me to convert and raise Catholic children. "You know, this priest I feel good about lives in Chicago. I want you to talk with him sometime," he told me. I was in no hurry and I'm sure he sensed my hesitation. It tugged at me because it seemed I would be giving up my own traditions as though they had never existed. My showing no interest in accompanying him to mass or visiting his priest any time soon should have triggered some discussion, but it didn't.

One afternoon out of the blue, Frank and Alice, the couple who had taken me in during my confinement, called to say they were in Ann Arbor.

"Your letter said you love Ann Arbor. We're so happy for you. You know Frank went to school here, so we are in for an alumnus gathering. Can we drop by for a visit?"

"Of course, please come. My apartment is in one of the dorms."

It was a warm visit. As we sat around having coffee, chatting about my new life in Ann Arbor, Jim appeared in the doorway. Not sure how to introduce Frank and Alice,

I stumbled through an introduction. "Jim, come meet some old friends of the family who are visiting Ann Arbor," I said. Jim stayed a while, charming them with his boyish smile and easy way of connecting with people. I knew they would not mention Ann, but I was on pins and needles just the same.

I sat there thinking of all that had happened in just a few months. My life was moving on quickly, but the buried secrets were mine to live with. As I settled in next to Jim, they saw me beaming; satisfied smiles spread across their faces and they gently began their goodbyes. Alice winked as she left. Phew! I'd gotten through that small lie, but I was wondering if Jim would ask more about them later.

I never saw Frank and Alice again. During our visit they were protective of my feelings and never brought up Ann or any details of her adoption or her new family. That part was a closed book. They sensed it was time for baby Ann, her new family, and me to move on.

Finally, I was in a good place. While falling into the rhythms of campus life, I was also slowly falling in love and feeling very connected to Jim and my new life there.

"Why don't I come to Pittsburgh and meet your parents after this term?" he blurted out one night as I kissed him good night. He thought it was time. That was exciting.

I knew Jim would captivate my mom, but I wasn't sure how he would impress my no-nonsense dad. Dad understood ordinary people well, probably from all his hours hanging with his buddies at the bar. He would disappear every night to hang out with friends he called "Red," "Lefty," "Doc," and "Da Mayor." Jim was more cerebral. He liked to chew over current events or dig into nuances of the law he was studying. Jim had great people skills, and I thought he would be fine. But what would he think of Mom and Dad?

Once we arrived at my house, I could not help but feel the undercurrent of heightened anticipation. Mom kept fretting about every detail of our separate bedrooms. Once the four of us were seated around our dining table, there were awkward moments of them glaring at Jim. Remembering some of the strained conversations between Judy and Dad, I dreaded what topic he might spring on Jim. Instead, Dad just sat there quietly observing Jim without going to any controversial subjects. Mother fussed a bit too much in the kitchen about her pot roast—whether it was done just right or overcooked. She rushed into the kitchen concerned the meringue on the lemon pie would burn. Mom wasn't a very relaxing person to be around, and Jim sat there blinking. To put him at ease, I brought up the subject of President Kennedy, knowing he would be only too happy to launch into his praises of the new president. He suddenly became animated, talking as if he were teaching a history class.

Dad liked Jim, calling him a bright and likable guy—but later commented, "Why was Jim so nervous? He keeps blinking!"

I held hands with Jim incessantly that weekend, and the drive to the airport was painful. We both knew our final goodbye would be traumatic. We had spent so many hours of each day together and were now facing the summer apart. I clung to him at the gate, and we hugged as long as was decent in front of Dad.

He whispered, "I love you and will miss you so much. But we'll see each other soon." It was going to be a long summer. I slowly pulled away and watched him board the plane with tears in my eyes.

Predictably, as the summer dragged on, I missed Jim terribly. His frequent letters started to slow to a trickle. I was confused. Maybe he was just too busy to write.

He arranged for me to visit his tiny hamlet just north of Chicago in early July. I was so excited to finally see him. But from the moment I stepped off the plane at O'Hare, I noticed a difference in him. It was not the same magnetism as at our departure. His greeting was nothing like our goodbye kiss in Pittsburgh, where we clung to each other until I thought my heart would break. Now he seemed guarded. Was it the awkward distance of time gone by? Was it his dislike for big cities? The hustle and bustle of O'Hare seemed to jar him. At any rate, he seemed nervous. His eyes were blinking.

Once we arrived in his hometown, where he had taught high school, he was immediately more relaxed, He exuded ease walking around, as though insulated from that other noisy world. Absolutely everyone knew him by name and responded to his boyish smile when we walked down the street. Such a politician he was, with kind exchanges for everyone, even then. This town was his comfort zone.

His mother showered me with attention. She made her specialty, German chocolate cake, for my arrival. A simple woman similar to my own mother, she proudly brought out a scrapbook of Jim's life and accomplishments in that small town. She showed newspaper clippings covering his conversion and how local priests helped him get into the university. I realized, hearing these stories and seeing the clippings, that his conversion was a seminal moment in his life.

The next afternoon, while driving around the country roads on the edge of this hometown, Jim swerved to the side of the road and stopped. It was the first time we were really alone. It was exciting but I was a bit startled. He reached over and folded me into his arms then started fondling me more aggressively than he ever had. At first, I thought it was pent-up passion after a long absence, but he was being forceful in a way that wasn't usual for him. It felt more aggressive than loving. At that moment my body stiffened. This set off something in me, a kind of warning. Maybe subconsciously my body was remembering the sexual assault. It was a reflexive reaction on my part, more than even I expected. I was confused as to what to say.

When I pulled away, he said irritably, "That's right, flirtatious one minute and rejecting the next."

This was not the Jim I knew in Ann Arbor. I was so stunned that I just sat in silence. On that quiet country roadside, with the smell of freshly cut hay floating in through the window, and his warm body next to me, I'd anticipated his tenderness. The warmth he usually exuded had completely melted away. I had wanted nothing more than to be close to him and feel his juicy kisses. Instead, he revved up the engine and swerved away. It sent a shiver through me.

I was totally confused but didn't know what to say. Talking about tenderness and desire isn't easy. Nor did it feel like the right time to launch into my delicate story about sexual assault. He wanted a "good woman." And in this town, he was the well-publicized Catholic convert and football hero. The quiet that followed in the car that afternoon was deafening.

The next day it was as though nothing had happened. He seemed like his old self, holding my hand as we ran errands. I sat in the car outside his church while he was at confession—wondering what he had to confess. Then, he buzzed around picking up his shirts from the cleaners while introducing me to everyone who seemed important to him in town.

When I returned to Ann Arbor from my strange visit, I was confused. Jim was warm and loving but there seemed to be new fissures in our relationship.

Not hearing much from him after my return to Ann Arbor was puzzling. After weeks of no letters or calls, I was distressed in a way I had never known. My pain went deep inside. With a blood pressure that is usually 90 over 60, I don't usually boil over, but I am very easygoing and never explosive. Not hearing from Jim made me grow sad inside and eventually quite sick. I was experiencing nonstop stomach upsets, my vision was blurry, and my knees buckled with weakness. Unable to go to work, no one could figure out what I had, not even the Infirmary. At least I knew for sure it wasn't pregnancy.

After I'd missed a week of work, my boss came to check on me. "I can't figure out what's wrong with you. No fever, no flu, and yet you are so weak." When I finally did regain strength and walked out into the summer sun, I shielded my eyes with my hands against the fierce, bright light. Apparently, I had suffered a mild stroke. I had this same experience thirty years later, when I suffered a more serious stroke. That blinding sunlight was the clue — strokes cause dilated pupils. But, that summer and at that moment, I had no idea what was wrong.

There was still no word from Jim or letters announcing when he was returning to campus. He didn't even know how sick I had been.

As people started returning to campus, friends dropped by to see me. One couple had just returned from Greece, where my friend's husband Dick was on a research mission. As an archaeologist, he spent the summer reading inscriptions off of the Acropolis while his wife Janie, one of my dietitian friends, would bake apple pies and fried chicken if someone in Greece would take her into their kitchen and cook their cuisine for her. They were enthralling me with stories of their Greek summer. Later that night over wine I shared with them my concerns about Jim.

With the fall term about to start, I was not sure how I would react to Jim. Feeling a bit stronger physically, I staged a welcome-back party for a few close friends. Dick sat there softly strumming his guitar while spinning Greek tales when Janie dragged me out into the hall. Jim had arrived on campus early, unannounced, and was waiting in the hall to surprise me. He swept me up in his arms with hugs and embraces as though nothing had happened. It was so unexpected, but I was too mellow from the wine I'd been drinking to ask more serious questions. I was just happy to see him so ebullient.

The next morning on our walk, hand in hand as usual, he simply asked, "So, when are we getting married, Mer?" The question trailed off unanswered. I was too confused over his silence at the end of summer to answer.

"Why didn't you write? You know I was very sick a few weeks ago." He never explained it, other than "So busy," but it was obvious he wanted our relationship to go on as usual.

Over the summer I had learned I could do a year-long dietetic internship at the University of Michigan Medical Center there. Great. Finally, I could finish what I had set out to do one year before when pregnancy had dramatically flipped my life upside down. That summer I settled into a new rhythm in Ann Arbor while feeling more focused and purposeful. My internship was in sync with Jim's plans—one final year in law school for him and a one-year internship for me. It seemed perfect.

For this internship I had to move across campus to a sparse apartment complex near the hospital. The interns were to live in student housing on a stipend. This was a step down from my cozy apartment in the residence halls with a salary.

But, once involved in the program, that included being part of a team of interns and doctors making their medical rounds each morning, I was energized and exhilarated about my new learning opportunity. While the other dietetic interns eyed the young medical interns on our daily rounds, and some began dating junior docs, I had Jim and was emotionally content and secure for the first time since summer.

One episode that took place near the hospital could have shattered my life further. Walking to class by myself dressed in the official whites of the medical profession, I took a shortcut to the hospital. It was a misty morning and the path was not well traveled, but it would save time on a rainy day. My head was covered with a thin plastic rain hat tied under my chin, the kind you kept in your purse for days just like this. Because the plastic covered my ears, I did not sense someone coming up behind me. Suddenly I was grabbed from behind by someone wrapping both arms around my hips. I slipped out of his grip and swung around to confront a young twenty-something man with a frightening glassy stare. I instantly swung at him with my purse as hard as I could and kept flailing around until he backed up. When I found my voice I shouted, "What are you doing, you pervert? Go away. I am calling the police." He turned and ran. Shaking from this confrontation, I pulled myself together and continued on to class. I sat there shaken while reflecting on my powerful fast reaction. No longer the go-along girl, the one sitting in the back of the class or waiting for others to decide my activities, I had fundamentally changed. I was my own person and ever on guard.

Living across the city now, Jim's trek to my place was much longer, so we saw less of each other. Still very much a couple on campus. I continued going to the law quad gatherings, and

Jim was joining my new circle of interns from the hospital across campus.

One class that required a day trip into Detroit for a seminar with a well-known nutritionist is etched forever in my memory. It was a beautiful November day in 1963. That day turned out to be one for the history books. This perky, pretty nutritionist sat perched on a stool in her white lab coat smoking a pipe. We thought she presented a very sophisticated image. She left the room for a few minutes but when she walked back in her shoulders were hunched and she stood there looking down for what seemed like forever. Finally, gaining back composure, she said, "I don't know quite how to say this, (she paused and looked down and then with anguish continued) but President Kennedy has just been shot!"

I can still feel the collective gasp from the classroom and the lump that formed in my throat. Nothing like this had ever happened in my lifetime. A leader being shot simply cracked my fifties stability.

The ride back to Ann Arbor was filled with anxiety and tears as Walter Cronkite, on the radio, struggled to tell the country what had happened. "President Kennedy died at 1 p.m. Central time."

For us, the president's death was unreal. That day, November 22, is now etched in our collective memories. We stumbled back to Ann Arbor. Jim and the interns gathered in my apartment that night, glued to the TV. He held my hand as the harrowing details unfolded. We could not comprehend how something so sinister could happen. That was the closest we were that term, clinging together through that alarming experience.

Later, Jim wanted us to go into Detroit for a special evening out centered around a play he wanted to see. Unfortunately, it was a weeknight, and I was program chairman for an American Dietetic Association meeting that same night. The director of my intern program, Miss Stumpf, was moderating a panel, so I'd asked some dietitian friends, "Can you do me a huge favor and cover for me Tuesday while I go to Detroit with Jim?" They promised to arrange the meeting set-up with a tea service and so on. It seemed fairly straightforward to me, so Jim and I were off to Detroit. We began the evening with a dinner in Greektown. Sipping ouzo and eating moussaka in a boisterous Greek taverna was way more exciting than eating hospital fare. I was just thrilled to be with Jim, exploring the nightlife of Detroit.

The next morning, sitting in class, I was summoned to Miss Stumf's office. When I walked in, she was pacing the room, her hands behind her back. Miss Stumpf was over six feet tall and towered well over me while strutting in her starched white uniform. She sounded like her name and railed at me as soon as I walked in. "Miss Keller, you had a responsibility last night, did you not?"

"Well, yes, but I had the meeting covered," I answered.

"When you are in charge of any assignment, it is your responsibility to see every detail is covered," she bellowed. "You did not follow through. There was chaos. Is that what I have been teaching you?"

My lower lip was trembling.

"You also taught us to use *Drucker's Management by Objectives*. ... I was just delegating and thought my directions were clear."

"Well, they were not. The meeting setup was clumsy, the room was in disarray with too few chairs, and the panel was not welcomed properly. Miss Keller, you have a lot to learn about management!" A few tears trickled down my cheek. She watched without trying to comfort me. It was an awkward moment, a verbal lashing about responsibility.

It was harsh, but I never forgot her lesson. Being upbraided royally taught me a lesson. To this day, if I am chairing an event or in charge of any project, no detail is left in question. I am obsessive about getting every detail right. In spite of her gruff manner that morning, she did me a favor. She mentored me about management and the delegation of duties. Years later, we became professional friends, and eventually she was proud of me.

Although stealing off to Detroit with Jim was a cozy escapade, our relationship had started to fray one thread at a time. I didn't see as much of him as before. We were both very busy on opposite sides of campus and I guessed that counted for our unraveling.

My new professional life was broadening. A very remarkable woman gave me a bit of advice I tucked away. She was a very attractive woman presiding over the local American Association of University Women (AAUW) chapter meeting. Married with children and a career, she seemed to have it all. After the meeting we were chatting, and I asked, "How did you meet your husband, and how do you know if someone is right for you? What did you look for in a partner?"

"Don't worry about finding Mr. Right," she said. "Think about your own sense of self. Find a career or life that suits you. Someone will find you, and your lives will blend together." That was a remarkable new perspective for someone like me from the fifties. Most women of my day were adjuncts to men—corporate wives, or working to get their husbands through graduate school. "Become your own person, and he will find you."

Jim and I still weren't sleeping together, and embraces lacked the earlier passion and warmth. They were more routine, and we seemed to be in a kind of a holding pattern. His fault? My fault? I wasn't sure. But, when we visited Chicago for a weekend, along with several of his Notre Dame friends, that trip seemed to mark a slide in our relationship.

Everything about Chicago was thrilling to me—the screeching elevated trains, the soaring buildings, the sweeping lakefront with all the colorful spinnakers breezing by. Best of all, I loved the neighborhoods like Old Town surrounding Second City, the improv comedy club. As we walked around, I thought about what it would be like to live there.

We were staying the evening in the Southside Irish neighborhood of Bridgeport, home to Mayor Daley and other well-known Irish families. As guests of the parents of one of Jim's Notre Dame friends, we gathered in the kitchen of their traditional old stone home. I felt keenly aware of the solid structure not only of the house but the network of friendships within. The law students from Ann Arbor were connected in more ways than one. Many of their parents were prominent Chicago lawyers. Just now the guys were sharing colorful accounts of their parochial school experiences. The nuns' obsessions with girls and their patent leather reflective shoes wasn't just something the comedian George Carlin would say. George was known to rift on growing up in Catholic schools in his routine "I Used to Be an Irish Catholic." Those parochial school stories told by Jim's friends always made me feel like I wasn't part of the clan.

Our host's mother, Anna, was a formidable Irish woman. She reminded me of Miss Stumpf. A tall woman, she wore oxfords rather than dainty flats, and a sensible but not stylish dress. She welcomed the guys warmly while giving me a sideways glance. Meanwhile, my eyes roamed over the wood-paneled den while observing the floor-to-ceiling law books and the buttery but worn leather chairs. It had the smell of old wealth. Jim so aspired to this inner circle of privileged Notre Dame legal minds.

Anna offered up drinks while directing us to where we would be sleeping. I was one of the few women along and knew we would have separate bedrooms, but Anna insisted on showing me to mine.

"Here is the alarm clock, unless you want us to wake you for mass in the morning."

Mass in the morning? My worst nightmare.

We had had a fun evening at Second City, but the next morning when we all got up for Sunday mass, I was suddenly anxious. Anna was in her kitchen stirring a pot of oatmeal and engineering the boys to get ready. I cringed. Never having been to a mass, I was sure I would screw it up, not knowing when to kneel and when to stand when the bells rang. I decided to decline the invitation. Jim came into my room several times to see if I would change my mind. Never having been to church with Jim, I didn't feel like making my debut here and now. I'm sure it didn't go down well in that Irish household.

He kept asking, "Are you sure you don't want to go?" .

I could tell that my response—"No, you go with them; I want to skip church today"—was like a dagger to his heart. The look on his face said that I had embarrassed him in front of his Notre Dame friends.

Back in Ann Arbor, I was still thinking about Chicago—the abundant energy, the skyscrapers, and the fun nightspots like Second City. I mulled over what kind of work I might find there.

A few weeks later a friend of mine, just back from a food convention in Chicago, came charging into my room. "Hey, a trade magazine is looking for a food editor in Chicago!"

"Did you apply?" I asked, since she was a dietitian as well.

"I gave them my card."

Weeks went by and she hadn't heard back. Meanwhile, I pictured myself in Chicago, working for a magazine. Hospital work was very routine; this would be much more exciting. Looking to relocate anyhow, I felt this was worth a try.

After first asking my friend once again if she was going to reapply, and hearing her say no, I hastily sent off my resume to the magazine. Within a few days a telegram arrived: "Please arrange to come for an interview at our editorial offices in Chicago as soon as possible. An airline ticket will follow."

The position was that of food editor for the leading restaurant and hotel trade magazine in the country, called *Institutions* magazine. It would be the most perfect career move I could imagine. Somehow, I had the chutzpah to think I could get the job.

Buzzing with excitement, I ran to the hospital cafeteria to find my friends, waving the telegram like it was a flag. I found Janie first and read it to her. She thought it was brilliant.

"If Dick was not working on his Ph.D., we would move to Chicago, too. Lucky you! Go for it!"

The other interns were happy for my prospect as well. We were all on the last leg of our internships and looking into career possibilities. This could be fantastic.

I then ran across the street to my friend June's apartment. While the interns lived in student housing, June, already established in the field, had a more gracious apartment. Many evenings I would plop down on her sofa and reveal bits and pieces of my fraying relationship with Jim. When detailing my recent trip to Chicago and my faux pas in refusing to go to mass, she said, "But, you two are perfect together. You will sort it out."

"June, I just landed an interview in Chicago with the magazine. They want me there for an interview as soon as possible. I haven't a clue what to wear. What do you think?" Eventually we leafed through issues of *Mademoiselle*, looking for fashion statements. We thought I should look professional but stylish.

On the day of the interview, I arrived wearing a tailored white silk shirt, a sleek black pencil skirt, fake alligator pumps, and scarab bracelets borrowed from June. I was going on intuition. It was a sophisticated magazine, and I wanted to project confidence with a smack of professionalism. But while I looked the part, I had a serious case of stage fright. Would I be what they were looking for?

Just stepping out of the taxi, I was in awe. Instead of arriving at an office building in Chicago's Loop somewhere, I was staring at an historic mansion that looked like it was right out of an English novel. Later I learned it was built for the Kimball piano family in 1892. This stately gated mansion with mansard roof was enchanting. To think—I just might be working in a castle.

Inside was an equally gracious interior with walls sheathed in onyx and a great hall two stories high. Today, there are tours of this elaborate mansion, but in 1964, it housed Medalist Publications. With no previous writing experience, I knew being hired as an editor was a very long shot. But after seeing this physical setting, I now desperately wanted the job.

After a brief tour around this grand mansion, it was time to meet the man himself, the publisher. When I was guided into his highly varnished office, I could smell the lemon polish and almost see my reflection in the gleaming wood panels.

An ornately carved fireplace framed his mahogany desk. The room was so grand that I guessed it must have been the Kimballs' living room. As I strode across the carpet to greet him, the first thing I noticed was his thin gray hair combover. He projected a sort of fatherly first impression. Sitting behind that impressive desk, he seemed small and not intimidating as

I had feared. After standing to greet me, he sat down, sinking even deeper into his leather chair, fingertips touching in a contemplative manner.

I had done my homework and quickly read *The Years with Ross*, about the eccentric founder of *The New Yorker* and the lofty visions he had for his magazine. Realizing how Ross extracted perfection from editors with blustering tirades, I was expecting some serious grilling.

He seemed softer than I anticipated but had the potential for being quirky. His hands gestured in a rather affected manner as he invited me to sit closer to him. After introductions and chitchat, I felt his penetrating gaze and he got right to the point. "What have they taught you in Ann Arbor about innovations in the food industry?"

I knew it was a loaded question, sort of *What do you know that we do not?* Also, he was gauging how quickly I would be able to shape an answer, while probing at what I would bring to the table. Did he not know I was mainly trained in hospital dietetics, tailoring diets for sick patients?

This was my big chance. I had to answer authoritatively. I do not remember what I answered, but he seemed satisfied. Then, he went on talking about the creative pool of talent at the magazine, giving several thumbnail sketches of editors and their awards. From the corner of my eye I could detect a sort of frenetic activity in the background. Outside his office, editors bustled about laughing and shouting out their lunch plans to see who wanted to join them. "We're going to Uno's; who's coming?" The spirited energy here was very unlike academia or the hospital where I'd interned. It all held the promise of excitement. But I was not sure my writing skills would garner any attention.

After meeting the inscrutable publisher, I was handed off to the food editor I was to be replace. Jane was a lofty, good-looking blonde in her early thirties. She exuded professionalism with her glasses pushed up on her forehead. She sat at her desk proofing galleys. "Be with you in a minute. We have this deadline to meet." I looked around her office at the stacks of magazines in disarray, old coffee cups, and a coatrack overloaded with umbrellas with assorted boots underneath. On her desk were photos of a sweet young boy. She had it all, career, family and husband. I admired her already.

One magazine on the stack caught my eye. I went over to examine the brilliant food photography more carefully, and she commented, "That shoot was challenging. We had to catch flaming crepes at just the right moment."

I just had to have this job, but how would I ever learn all she knew about food photography, proofing galleys, and directing a shoot?

Jane was moving up to managing editor when she returned from maternity leave. Here was an accomplished editor with a degree in journalism. How would she assess me and my nascent writing skills? My knees started shaking.

I wasn't surprised when she said, "Here are some notes from an interview I had with the chef at Jacques French restaurant. This is their menu with bits and pieces of conversation about their history and popular dishes. Write me a sample article, just a page or two," and then she left me alone in her office. The opening sentence was a challenge. Scanning her notes, an opening sentence soon came to me, and once I had that down, I began to weave sentences together laced with food descriptions that seemed to naturally flow from me. I was so glad that I had read food magazines so often.

Handing her my copy, I scrutinized her face looking for signs of a response. As she sat reading my copy, she tapped the paper with her pencil making small marks. Was she editing? I sat patiently waiting for her reaction, sweating profusely now through my shirt. Slowly a smile started to break across her face. Setting the paper aside, she said, "Let's get some lunch while I show you our neighborhood." Those were words of encouragement. My spirits were soaring as we walked out to lunch.

That copy test, along with my impending new credentials as an ADA dietitian, seemed to seal the deal. Over lunch, Jane offered me the job as food editor, a prime spot on the masthead even though I had never written food copy before. What a high for me after so many lows. Bursting with excitement, I hardly heard the condition that I needed start as soon as possible. Jane needed to train me before she went on leave.

Now I had to get permission to leave the internship for a few weeks. If they agreed, I would need to hastily pack my bags and move quickly into a whole new life, the world of publishing in a dynamic city like Chicago.

My earliest image of the city was gleaned from my English lit classes. The brawny city of big shoulders was also known for organized crime, the violence of Al Capone, and political corruption. Nelson Algren's *Chicago, City on the Make,* and Theodore Dreiser's *Sister Carrie*, all set in Chicago, made me a bit apprehensive about stepping onto this new stage. Nelson grappled with the soul of the city, the hustlers, the politics, the beauty, and the passion. Carrie in *Sister Carrie was* the small-town girl, seduced by the suave city slicker, Drouet. She was in a city she didn't comprehend. As it was for Carrie, this was a new whole game for me. But, I had already experienced the vagaries of life and had toughened up a bit.

I also had to face the fact that Jim and I had slowly drifted apart. My career seemed to be taking off swiftly, but our once-special love wasn't so special. Our incessant hand-holding had faded away and I wasn't exactly sure why. Looking back, we never addressed the deeper issue in our relationship, like the religion that apparently was so important to him, or my secret. By not going to mass or taking instructions with his priest, I had probably caused him some heartburn. Why should I have to abandon my religion and let priests raise my kids? Remembering the long robes of the nuns visiting my childhood friend's house, I recalled that their dangling crucifixes made me cringe. Religion was one roadblock, but there were others.

Our relationship had just flamed out. I knew our intimacy never evolved as it should have. Pete had not only stolen my dignity but left me with intimacy issues as well. I paid the price of silence.

Thinking Jim would never accept my story, my secrets stayed buried. I was still too raw. It had just been a short while since I went through the wrenching experience of kissing Ann goodbye, and I felt his empathy quota was not large enough to walk in my shoes. I was supposed to be the "good woman."

Yet, it would be hard to just walk away from a relationship that had held so many tender moments. I missed the notes under my door as our relationship blossomed. Now, we shared a respect for each other—just no longer a deep love. In many ways Jim was the ideal man—handsome, focused, and charming to everyone he met. We had had many magical times, but we were no longer in sync.

One of the most confusing nights of my life was the one when Jim came to see me for a final goodbye as he headed home from graduation. I had started working with the magazine a few weeks before his graduation and was staying in a downtown Chicago hotel, the magazine's idea, until I could find an apartment. The Sherman House was a noisy convention hotel anchored in the loop near the screeching sounds of elevated train tracks. I felt alone and alienated in that setting. It was to be temporary, but spending each night in a hotel room was anything but a comfortable experience. Jim had just graduated law school and planned to come by the hotel that night on his way back home. We both knew there was a finality to this meeting.

After work, I strolled to the hotel, wondering how the evening would end. Would we discuss now what had gone wrong? As I walked along State Street, sailors loitered on street corners, eyeing the passing women. The images of this muscular city that Dreiser had written about so eloquently swept into my thoughts. I wondered how I would ever adapt to this boisterous city of broad shoulders after small college town life.

This large convention hotel was a cold, impersonal setting for our final parting. It was pretty clear we were going our separate ways, but he came anyway. It had been such a sweet beginning that the "goodbye" would be hard. Not knowing what to expect, when he gently knocked, I opened the door. He bent down and kissed me. Then, an awkward silence followed. I sat down on the bed and started jabbering about my crazy times at the magazine, including the new bosses and office escapades. He sat there listening and chatting for a while, then went silent. He came over and pulled me up to him, and held me for a long time, just stroking my hair. Neither of us said anything. We had shared so many warm moments together, and I imagined they were floating through both of our memories. Neither of us had words at that moment.

Then his hand ran down my thigh, pulling up my skirt. Why now? It wasn't like him. Very tenderly but deliberately he started to make love. I was confused. We had gotten to this point before and stopped, but he wasn't stopping now. Passion was the last thing I could summon from my emotions that were mostly a mix of sadness and confusion. Desire was muted. I didn't feel like throwing myself into a sizzling love scene to save something that just wasn't there.

I hadn't expected this. Maybe he was trying to leave me with a taste of what could have been. To me, it seemed shabby.

Too much had watered down our initial infatuation. An act of love at this point was more like a candle being extinguished than ignited. For him, it may have been more a conquest, a rape? Later in life I reflected on this scene. It was like the Rashomon effect, based on the old Japaese movie Rashomon, where each person has contradictory conclusions to an event. In any case, it was a goodbye I was not anticipating.

After this awkward act, he left with few words. I sank down on a bed that had probably been the site of many scorching romances or one-night stands. That hotel room was hardly the place for our once-sweet relationship to end. I felt deeply sad he chose to end it by forcing himself on me.

Through silent tears I wondered why he decided to use sex as his parting shot. It wasn't going to seal anything. Maybe it was more an act of resentment than an act of love. He just tiptoed off into the night.

I sat on the bed dazed, my mind and emotions thrashing around. It was not a loving farewell. It was dishonest. Sex without emotion is cheap. What was he trying to say?

The curtain was not fluttering down like it did in the finale from *La Bohème*. Mimi may have died from pneumonia, but she was cherished, and Rodolfo wept. I felt the tragedy of a lost love, lost sometime way before that night.

Chapter Twelve
Reflections Before Dawn

Feeling wounded and confused about the price of my silence with Jim, I stayed awake thinking about more tender intimacies from my past. My thoughts drifted back to my very first love in high school senior year.

Bryce had social skills beyond his age because he was an Army brat and used to fitting in fast wherever his family lived. Adults, especially parents, loved him. When his family first came to town, his stylish mother with her pink pillbox hats and his pipe-smoking West Point dad had caused quite a stir. Bryce charmed everyone and especially me. One year older, more worldly, he seemed suave compared to classmates my age. Soon, we were going steady and spending enormous amounts of time together.

I was intrigued by his mother. She would often ask me to stay for dinner and would probe a bit at my plans for college. When I told her I would probably end up as a dietitian, she asked, "Have you ever thought of journalism? You could become a writer."

I thought to myself, how many jobs would there be for a journalism major when dietitians are needed everywhere? But, she had planted the seed. One could do or become many different things.

Bryce and I grew into intimacy sweetly and slowly. Soon we were peeling back the layers of our budding sensuality at drive-in theaters, or on secluded backroads with the car windows steaming up to Johnny Mathis's "Chances Are" drifting from the radio. Our passions hit a crescendo that brought me a flood of tears and a bolt of emotion. That was such a sweet first sensual journey.

After Jim left that night, I compared his abrupt foray with that sweet experience with Bryce.

Not sleeping a wink, I brooded for hours over that sad finale. It felt like a divorce. Tears were streaming down my cheeks. Finally, I sat up to watch the dark night shadows receding over that brawny city. The silhouettes of tall buildings were slowly emerging. The cityscape was both frightening and promising. Was I really ready to start over yet again?

As the city was coming to life, the whistles and cat calls from the street below were replaced with sounds of the elevated train rumbling by, bringing workers into the city. The early-morning sky was suddenly streaked with a sliver of uplifting crimson brilliance. A sunrise held the promise of a new beginning. A sign of hope. Here I was, yet again, starting over in a city where I barely knew a soul. I took a deep breath and shoved down pain once again. I was ready for a new twist to my kaleidoscope.

Chapter Thirteen

A New Beginning

————— ∿∿ —————

Slowly I began adjusting to the drama swirling around me in this dazzling city. Life in the early sixties in Chicago was so thrilling, I had little time to lick wounds or revisit pains of the past.

With Lincoln Park at my doorstep, each morning I would step outside my high-rise, then turn east towards my bus stop on Lake Shore Drive, the windiest corner in all Chicago. Walking there through ice and slush my first winter, my high heels would sink into mush; my thin wool coat could not begin to repel the slashing winds. I clung to the corner lamppost for balance. Just waiting for my bus to the south side, I could be chilled to the bone. This was the Windy City, after all.

One particular summer morning, as I walked to my bus, passing the elegant old homes on Astor Street, I tried to imagine the grand lives that took place in those stately mansions built by Louis Sullivan and Frank Lloyd Wright after the great Chicago fire. Not only was I lucky to be living in this historic neighborhood in the Near North, but I was heading to work on the South Side to yet another historic district, the Prairie Avenue District. It was home to the grand mansions of Marshall Field and other Chicago aristocrats. Working in that old Kimball Piano mansion was a heady experience.

I smiled to myself as I walked along that day, thinking about my good fortune to be here, living and working among these impressive reminders of Chicago's halcyon years. At age twenty-three, I felt blessed. A huge leap from just a few months ago, when my future was tossed up in the air.

Like a magnolia unfolding its petals in the warmth of summer sun, I slowly opened up to a new life in a pulsating city. Leaving behind the dictums of the straightlaced fifties, I was walking straight into a vibrant new decade, the psychedelic sixties. For me, it was a brilliant awakening.

Each morning as I entered that old mansion, it was magical, like entering another era. Passing through the wrought-iron gate, I was always in awe of the gingerbread architecture, the polished wood panels, and the dramatic stairways. Inside, I was adjusting to the daily intrigue of office politics.

Pushing away thoughts of Jim and a marriage that had never materialized, I focused now on my work. My job was exhilarating but also daunting. I had to learn skills I did not yet have to navigate the inner workings of this perplexing new world of publishing.

Among those challenges was to learn all about food photography. Once I had a concept for the food shot, I knew it had to be styled by the art department. The props, location, and authentic representation of the icy cold or flaming food was my part of the process. I had a lot to learn to just grasp the inner workings of the art department. I would tiptoe softly into the department to plead my case with the art director for a double-page spread. He terrified me at first. Knowing that he had skillfully staged many shoots for the magazine and their professional books, in this art department he was king. With wildly waving hands, this short Greek man with a passionate personality, deeply penetrating eyes, and bushy eyebrows could be very intimidating. He would abruptly cut me off mid-sentence, but he was also a creative genius. It was nerve-racking trying to weave through his zany antics just to make my pitch.

"I need at least a two-page spread to capture that lavish Scandinavian smorgasbord at Kungsholm."

"Says who? What do you know about creating layout drama, huh? You know nada." It took me awhile to understand that his put-downs were done in jest.

I also needed to learn the politics of ad placement within the magazine format to keep our sales reps and their advertisers happy. My own preemptive move was to create a calendar of my intended feature articles so our space reps had plenty of time to pitch their placement. Publishing was a business, and I was absorbing how it all worked.

In due time, I was more confident walking into the art department, but each corner of that publishing house had its own idiosyncrasies. I had to work through the personality quirks and territorial posturing.

One of the more flamboyant editors, who had a penchant for canary-yellow shirts, had on his desk a giant teacup the size of a soup bowl. "Johanna, come refill my tea," he would roar. Sitting behind his desk, with dramatic sweeping gestures he would lift his cup and peer over it before beginning any conversation. He was not the only eccentric there. I did feel like I had fallen down the rabbit's hole into a new world of office antics and games you simply had to play.

The older editors, in their forties, were a crusty crew with sharp tongues and constant witticisms. They would sit around casting themselves as characters in a popular Broadway show, choosing the glamorous role each would like to play.

One senior editor leaned back in her chair and said, "I see myself as Gloria Swanson, with her sleek cigarette holders, long gloves, and diamond bracelets." She turned to me and said, "Who would you be?" Before even answering she offered, "Maybe Alice in Wonderland?" I guess my naiveté was showing. I was the quiet, polite one, not the zany wisecracker.

Office politics aside, working for the magazine was intoxicating. In just a few short months I had gone from small-town experiences to covering national food trends, running stories on the jazzy new restaurants and the chefs behind them. The magazine also worked with the Culinary Institute of America to publish the first *Professional Chef,* the bible for the culinary world. With striking food photography staged by our art director, it depicted step-by-step procedures of classic preparations. These beautifully illustrated pages became a training manual for chefs. It was exciting to watch them build a book of such prestige and be in the middle of a burgeoning new trend in food preparation.

Traveling for the magazine was the biggest adrenaline rush. I had to pinch myself to believe this was real. Boarding each flight, I would watch in wonder as the buildings in Chicago shrank beneath me to toy-sized when the plane left the runway. It was hard to believe the magazine was actually paying me to fly around the country, meet industry leaders, visit culinary schools, and attend conferences. I was beginning to feel the year that I suffered in silence was finally behind me. My role as food editor put me in the center of a world of extraordinarily creative chefs, restaurateurs, and hoteliers. It was fulfilling my wildest dreams.

Even better, I often traveled to cities where I could reconnect with friends, and especially my close sorority sisters.

Visiting them in their row houses in Philadelphia or lofts in Boston, I loved to hear about their new lives and skillfully left out the grim realities of my lost year. However, they were filled with awkward questions.

When I met Janet in Boston, one of the first things she asked was, "What happened? We lost track of you."

"I did my internship in Michigan instead of New York," I said, but never elaborated on the fact that it was months later. I doled out partial truths to protect myself and my very real, raw story.

"So, you were there over a year and you never wrote?"

"Well, I was all involved with extra study at the university and off in my own world," I said, hoping she wouldn't ask any more questions. I quickly changed the subject.

In New York I re-connected with my friend June from my Ann Arbor days. She had artfully coached me on the proper look for my job interview. June's assessment of style was her métier. Now shopping in Manhattan with June, we spent weekends combing through designer discount houses as well as every floor of Bloomingdales for stylish outfits. Shortly after, I was maid of honor at her wedding.

At the rehearsal dinner, her mother asked me, "Whatever happened to that handsome lawyer friend of yours from Ann Arbor? He was so charming, and you were perfect together."

That made me wince. My memories and a Jim lingered. Wanting to suddenly know more about him, I called Ann, a friend from Ann Arbor who was living just down the street from me in Chicago. Ann had been dating one of the Notre Dame guys Jim knew well. She would know. I tried to veer casually into the topic, asking, "Do you ever see Jim or hear about him?" Her answer floored me.

"Jim is getting married."

I clenched my fist so hard I dug my nails into the palms of my hand until they stung.

"Well," I asked, "who is she, and what is she like?"

"A hair stylist in his hometown. I think she might have been a student in his history class when he was teaching."

I asked if he ever mentioned me, and she said, "He did say that his regret was not to have married you when you were first in love."

Now I put it together. He had been seeing her all along. That summer that changed everything suddenly came into focus. He had been dating her the summer I visited—playing the field on his home turf. That was a jolt. I still had the baggage of memories and a sweet love that just drifted away.

To make me feel better, I rationalized that ours was just a campus fling and that we were not really in sync on several levels. I sensed he didn't have the empathy capable of relating to me or my story. He was more a politician, trying to curry favors even on campus. His real comfort level was being a small-town lawyer, and eventually he did become mayor of his town. I, on the other hand, was thriving in my new pulsating urban environment.

My life had evolved into a fast track of work with flamboyant chefs, tracking food styles, and the surging new ethnic restaurants. Dressing in suits by day, cocktail dresses for evening receptions, and various outfits for travel, my days were deliciously exciting. The trade junkets I attended for the country's magazine and newspaper food editors were extraordinary events. In Colorado we rode horseback to a bubbling stream where they pulled out fresh trout to be grilled for breakfast. There were extravaganzas sponsored by the public relations arms of organizations for the grand dames of

Good Housekeeping, Gourmet, Better Homes and Gardens, House Beautiful, etc. One of these editors took me under her wing by suggesting I round out my career by moving to Paris. But, I was not ready for yet another disruption. I was more interested in planting roots and finding a new love to replace Jim. It seemed I just wasn't meeting many exciting men my age.

One sweltering hot summer night, trudging home with my briefcase loaded with work, I saw in the distance a group of friends casually lounging on the doorstep of their brownstone. I was envious of this carefree social scene. As I drew closer, I could hear laughing and then recognized Ann as one of them.

"Hey, Meredith. Want a cold beer?" I sat down and chatted for a while. Jealous of this relaxed setting, wishing I could stay longer, I exchanged a few words and just kept walking home to face yet another evening burning the midnight oil. I was longing for more companions my own age, but I had a deadline to meet and wanted to reflect on a new dilemma at work that day.

Our managing editor, Jim, had invited me to lunch out of the blue. This snowy-haired gentle man, more reserved than the rest, spoke softly but with a slight stutter. Some of the junior editors would mimic him behind his back, but they respected him. At lunch at a posh restaurant, Jim quickly ordered his martini, and soon after another. He seemed a bit nervous and the stutter became apparent. I gathered he was bracing himself to tell me something. Maybe he was going to fire me?

"Meredith, I don't think you are aware of this, but someone is after your job."

"OK, who is it? Someone from another magazine?"

His eyes lowered like he wasn't sure he should say who it was. Then, he said, "Judy, that pain in the ass, always wanted your job. She was upset she was not promoted to food editor when you were appointed."

I remembered Judy coming late to the office one day, close to lunch time. When Jim asked why she was late, she said, "I have my period and it made me feel all crampy and headachy. It's a girl thing."

She knew how to embarrass Jim into silence.

"The kicker is," Jim went on to tell me, "she is also sleeping with Bill." (Bill was the publisher). "She can make trouble but, never mind. ... I think I can help here."

"Does everyone know?"

"A few know, and they are very annoyed. She is a clever one. Here is what you do. She writes snappy headlines, so ask her to help you with yours. Keep your enemies close."

"Won't she think this is proving what an asset she can be?"

"She will think she is gaining power by helping you. Meantime, I will try to find another spot for her and another title. It is going to be a bit tricky."

When Jim ordered his second martini, I did as well. Back in the office, I had to put my head on the desk to recover. Drinking to glean information or protect your job was getting challenging.

Life in that crazy mansion would make a great sitcom—sex, lies, and loads of alcohol. There was intrigue about who could get away with coming in late, what editors were lunching with whom, who was having closed-door meetings with the publisher, who would get the lead story, who had the ear of the art director to get the splashiest layout, and who was the most entertaining. Sorting through the after-work shenanigans became as taxing as my daytime work.

Absorbing these office intrigues, I tried to keep a safe distance from the publisher. Although much respected in the industry, I had noticed his lecherous behavior. Yet, he kept all of us on our toes with editorial contests and critiques, and he even graded our work on occasion. Under his tutelage, I learned to sharpen my pen, but I kept my distance.

I soon realized he was also capable of teaching me valuable life lessons. He coached me not just on my writing skills but the needed social skills for business. At my very first industry cocktail party, when I was dressed in a long gown for a formal reception at the Huntington Hartford Gallery in New York, he came over to me and said, "I want you to go into this room tonight and come out knowing the five most important industry leaders. Learn how to circulate. Don't be a wallflower. I will be watching you."

That was a big challenge for this small-town girl. I needed to stretch to meet yet another new situation. I stood tall and looked around for a likely path to take in my new task of circulating a room. It wasn't so hard. I targeted a small gathering and found how to use my new professional powers. "Hi, I am Meredith, the new food editor at the magazine, what is your company, again?" They were more than happy to talk with me, bring drinks, and soon turn into lecherous men. The publisher also guided me on what to do about that without being offensive. "Remember, many of them are our biggest advertisers."

It wasn't the only advice he gave me. I respected him and feared him at the same time. His womanizing ways didn't stand in the way when he gave me direct personal advice. One evening as he was driving me home from the South Side along the Outer Drive in full view of Chicago's impressive skyline, with all the dazzling lights from the skyscrapers flashing and sparkling, he turned and said, "This city can be yours. It is there for the taking, and it is up to you to take advantage of it. Go for it!"

I didn't know until years later that he suffered from delusions of grandeur. He bought a mansion he could ill afford on Astor Street and staged industry conferences that were over-budget extravaganzas. But to me, at age twenty-four, having someone tell me to reach for the moon, that it was within reach, was very heady stuff. Crazy as he might have been, he was a great publisher and mentor.

These late-night bacchanalias flowed from the office into night. The group carried their "fun and games" into someone's apartment or nearby restaurants. Never wanting to be the first to leave these alcohol-laced events for fear they would talk about me, I stayed trying to keep a cool reserve, watching from the sidelines.

After a few years in this circus-like atmosphere, I yearned for the normal life, like my friends sipping beer on the steps of their brownstone after work had. Imagining life outside that zany publishing house, I was ready for a nine-to-five workplace.

Chapter Fourteen

Winds of Change

———~~———

The mid-sixties felt like a thunderbolt. There was a vital energy in the air as the sexual and cultural revolutions emerged with tangible fury. The streets were dramatically charged with political and social turmoil. These were enlightening times but confusing times for someone like me, raised in the quiet conformity of the small-town fifties. Especially after living through the consequences of sexual assault, these new freedoms excited me but kept me cautious.

The birth control pill had just arrived, freeing up sexual passions. I felt stuck in a gray area somewhere between the *Father Knows Best* era of my teens and the new bra-burning sixties I was now living through. I was thankful for the pill, which kept women from having to pay the heavy price I did. But the "free love" of the era seemed to me to be going too far. Dating quite a bit now, I found myself restrained about intimacy. I was firmly in the yellow caution zone and not allowing myself deep entanglements. Although I became freer about sex than I'd been with Jim, I was no longer a trusting soul around men. That sexual assault stayed with me.

Observing all the social turmoil over the war in Vietnam, you could not miss the growing dissonance between generations; young people proudly flashing peace signs versus the scowling "Love it or leave it "older group. The generation gap was widening, so I decided to bring my conservative dad to Chicago to experience the vibes in Chicago. Actually, I felt I was secretly challenging him about his attitudes, as Judy had often done. How would that go? I loved my Dad, missed him, and was grateful for all he had done for me. I was going to be respectful. Mostly, I wanted him to see the positive changes in me and that I was more than OK.

Almost immediately, Dad was in awe of Chicago. Our scenic boat ride on Lake Michigan to look back at the skyscrapers impressed him. But that didn't interest him as much as the many ethnic neighborhoods. I introduced him to bodegas and bars serving enchiladas, pierogi, or schnitzel ... and lots of beer. Not surprisingly Dad was most comfortable in the bar scene. I had never been in a bar with Dad, so at first it felt a bit odd. Although he left our family most nights to take a seat at his local hangout, we never saw his more gregarious side firsthand. He immediately relaxed. It was his milieu as he bantered with bartenders.

Showing Dad my Chicago was just plain fun. "Look who is coming for lunch, too," he said gleefully, pointing out a cockroach crawling over the table in one of the more charming but not-so-clean spots in Old Town. He was happy to peek into my new life. I was curious to see his reaction to the activity on the streets.

Dad kept his own hair well shorn, routinely visiting his barber Sam, where local gossip was exchanged. He told me, "In barber chairs, men grumble about the long-hairs protesting the war." I knew the scene here would set Dad's hair on fire. As we walked the streets, I heard him say, "It's every man's duty to serve his country."

A few years later the Broadway musical *Hair* was this in-your-face rebuke to conservative parents like mine. The street scene I introduced to my dad in the sixties was shocking for him, but not to me anymore. I, too, was changing.

He heard the electrifying lyrics fanning the flames of the drug culture. The Beetles "I Get High with a Little Help from My Friends" was blaring from bars. The scent of marijuana was everywhere, wafting through theaters, parks, and concerts.

Demonstrations around the city were common. The most impactful for me was when women hit the streets to march for women's rights. These were not just youthful mini-skirted twenty-somethings, but also older women who stepped out of the shadows of their past to march. I admired these courageous women, who fought for women's rights and abortion rights. When I thought back to the pain and humiliation I had suffered, I was so proud of them.

Bob Dylan was reminding us that the times were "a-changin'." For me, these were energizing times. Provocative times. Music was in the air and under my skin. Drug-laced sex was the new wave, but not for me. I still felt vulnerable and very much in risk-avoidance mode when it came to men and sex.

Janis Joplin, just three years younger than me, also from a small town, was experiencing a freer, more uncorked life than mine. She was singing her heart out in Haight-Asbury in San Francisco with "Freedom is just another word for nothing left to lose." Those words held a message for me. I could not just abandon myself like Janis. Her raspy voice belted out lyrics with such abandon. I loved her style, but instead of feeling "nothing left to lose," I felt I had everything to lose, again.

By contrast, I thrived under the conventions she rebelled against. Leaving the magazine to find a saner life, I joined the corporate world as publicist for Armour and Company. This move was the totally opposite scene from the zany publishing house. Being a corporate insider seemed like safer territory.

I was now gravitating toward professional organizations, networking and moving forward on a sound career path. I wanted stability. Men could wait. I remembered the advice of the woman in Ann Arbor who said to follow your own talents and men will find you—no need to chase them. Men were not my main focus, although I always had dates. With the sting of a lost love and a lost child, I was in no rush to throw my life into chaos.

Feeling I had "everything to lose," I kept my cards close to my chest, never revealing that bad hand I had been dealt. I kept silent but also wondered if Pete ever thought for a minute of what he had put me through. Did he ever stop to think about the child he had fathered?

Continuing on my networking path, I joined the Junior League, more or less just like I had joined a sorority. It was a prestigious group, mostly wives of the captains of industry, and known for their high-profile charitable work. When I joined, I was one of the very few career women in the group. Networking under crystal chandeliers in their grand old estate on Astor Street, I thought of myself not as part of the social scene, but as a voyeur. "So, this is how wealthy young women spend their time," I thought. Feeling a bit like a mouse in the corner, I watched these women, with nicknames like "Boots" and "Candy," sipping sherry and mingling in this fashionable brownstone, prancing about in expensive Chanel suits and dangling Gucci purses.

This felt very different from operating in the corporate world. Business had clear-cut rules and protocols for achieving goals. In the Junior League, as in other private organizations of the time, money, and power played an important role. It was a different game than I had ever witnessed. But I was not intimidated. By observing their ways, and joining their ranks, I became the co-chair of a program that made them spend more than they had ever spent on an urban outreach program.

My project centered on drug abuse, a huge issue of the day, with a teen drop-in drug center. The challenge was to train these Junior League volunteers in drug therapy technique so they could understand the scene where they would volunteer time.

We hired a very hip, savvy women. She was an ex-junkie and an ex-prostitute, as well as a very street-smart woman. Pockmarked and a bit sassy, with salty language to match, Ellen was the perfect person with the right skillset for the job A bit coarse by Junior League standards, with her fuck-you language, Ellen had a unique expertise that we were about to experience.

Ellen walked into her first meeting with the volunteers, sized up the elegant living room full of perfectly coiffed volunteers, and decided training would begin that moment with an encounter session. As she walked around the circle of women, she asked each to "Tell something revealing about yourself."

She clarified: "I don't want to hear where you went to college, or about your husbands. I don't want stats. I want to know what makes you tick, what bothers you, what issues you might have. Reveal something personal and real about yourself."

The women seemed baffled but slowly opened up. It was riveting. I would not divulge my inner secret, but some women did. One pretty blonde dressed in a cerulean blue angora sweater that seemed to match her soft personality was next up. She was a picture of perfection, and we knew she lived in fashionable Lake Forest.

With her doe-like eyes tilted down, she began, "Well, the truth is I had to get married before college was over. Now I have two small children I adore at home, but my life is really very lonely. My husband ignores me and barely speaks to me. I dutifully pick him up each and every night at his 5:45 train. He pours a drink, then sits at the dining table reading his newspaper without even looking at me. It is a dreadful life. I was finally thinking I was strong enough to pull out of this marriage and find I am now pregnant again."

There was a quiet moment in the room, and then a wave of collective compassion that was palpable. We all immediately felt her pain. It went deep inside each of us. Her pain was also etched on our faces. What a revelation to watch how easily each of these women, so guarded by form and refined manners, could open up so emotionally and reveal themselves when simply asked. It went on in this vein around the room, each woman talking openly for the first time. Women who politely sipped sherry at meetings were talking about their anxieties. It was exactly what Ellen had wanted, full disclosure with insight.

Although I did not bare my real-life story, I couldn't help but think how lucky I was not to have been forced into marriage. Hearing this woman's story made me realize what a bullet I'd dodged. Marriage doesn't buy you out of a bad situation or guarantee you love or respect. She was miserable.

The dynamics in the room were gripping. We immediately bonded in a more real way. Ellen had made her point by demonstrating the foundation for group therapy. We felt its power in that morning session.

Later, when wives told our husbands about our unique "tell all" day, some male feathers were ruffled.

"I don't want our private lives spilling into someone's living room," some said. "You don't need to go to those sessions anymore."

Ellen then suggested something even more provocative. "Some of you should go to this counterculture retreat on the West Coast. It would further your experiences in sort of an unleashed learning environment." One woman in the group did go and came back to tell of bathing suit-optional pools and massages given by a topless woman.

She thought the experience was enlightening, but her husband did not. When she told him, he said, "I've spent many years defining and cultivating my life. That does not compute with my value system."

It was a royal smackdown from her husband. Apparently, some husbands felt threatened by Ellen's non-conventional training, even in the "If it feels good, do it" atmosphere. We snickered at the husband's comments but carried on. When our training sessions were over, we held a celebration dinner for Ellen, husbands included. We toasted her and thanked her "a fucking lot" for her salty language, insights, and unique training. She demonstrated the art of open communication to a group used to filtering their comments and emotions.

My main focus through these turbulent sixties was to just move through them. I was busy creating a new social and professional life that included having new men in it. I sought a way of life that was engaging enough to let me forget the previous bad chapters. In spite of Ellen's tutoring and the "Let it all hang out" attitudes around me, I was still pretty locked down about sharing my emotions or my stories. My secret was being buried even deeper.

Chapter Fifteen

The Encounter in 1966

One shocking incident stopped me in my tracks. While working at the magazine the other editors had mentored me well about the importance of networking. The older editors I observed were especially adept at making a stranger feel like their best friend. A little uncomfortable at first, I became nimbler at mingling and schmoozing with industry leaders at conferences and trade shows.

At one important industry conference, as I was working the McCormick Place Convention Center in Chicago, I suddenly felt eyes staring in my direction. Someone just across the aisle was sizing me up. At the time, I was chatting with one of the

convention's speakers and a good friend of the magazine's. Networking at its best. But, I had to know whose prying eyes were fixated on me.

When I finally looked over, I couldn't believe my eyes. There stood Pete, observing me from across the aisle. What a shock! I had never expected our paths to cross again. Without showing any signs of recognition, I kept talking to this other man. Did I have the stomach for this? Should I acknowledge Pete or ignore him? I had to make a snap judgment.

I bought some time by exchanging business cards and stretching out our conversation while I tried to figure out my next move. Should I shrug him off and pretend he didn't exist, that he wasn't standing there to be recognized? Should I walk right by and snub him? Would I have the courage to remind him of all I had been through? No, not here, not in this setting.

With surging confidence, I realized he was now on my turf. In that split second I looked up, I noticed he had struck the exact same pose as when I tried to confront him on campus about my pregnancy. He had that deer in the headlights stare, caught, but not yielding an inch. But I was ready.

Walking boldly over to him I said, "Pete, what brings you here?" as if this were my domain, not his. He had the same smirk he always had back in college.

He mumbled something about looking for products for his inn. "I just like to come here and see what's new."

He did not even offer a humble "How are you?" or fake bonhomie for an old classmate. Instead he seemed content to stand there and just intensely observe me as his eyes rolled over me. As he was sizing me up, I noticed those eyes expressed no recognition of me as the person for whom he had caused so much pain. I observed the same stone-cold stare. There was not a shred of empathy behind his eyes.

Before me I saw a thief. He had stolen a year of my life—robbed me of the normal expectations as a graduating senior. That single incident of his unsolicited sex had cost me dearly. I had to suffer shame and disappear to bear his child while his life went on. I spent years trying to reshape my life. Did he know about my tear-stained pillows from telling my proud parents just after graduation that I had a big problem to share? Did he know the personal price to my total being in handing my own child over for adoption? Did he feel any sense of participation in the emotional trauma that would linger my lifetime because of him?

I wasn't sure where to go with this awkward moment. It was unnerving. He didn't ask a thing about me or even offer a simple, solicitous, "How have you been?"

Seeking some safe ground to catch my breath, I started asking about other classmates we knew. As he rattled on, mentioning names, he still seemed to be that smug, all-knowing person I remembered from the past.

I sensed my body resisting him. It was tightening up, remembering the hold he once had over me. Because of him, my life had hit that devastating low, and he was the cause. My body was on guard.

But, while I retained a very calm facade, my stomach was churning. With my body now on high alert, I straightened up, wanting to project that I was in control now. Here he was seeing me face to face and didn't project one sympathetic tone in his voice. His cavalier retort —"I can get you pills for that"—when I told him about my pregnancy floated through my thoughts. His cold indifference hadn't changed a bit.

I kept wondering if he was ever going to ask the obvious questions: "Did I have a son or daughter?" "Do you have any details about the adoption?"

But he wasn't asking anything real about me and certainly wasn't getting even close to asking those questions. Wouldn't he like to know, even out of curiosity?

Despite his not asking about me, I finally inserted, "I'm a food editor now, with *Institutions Magazine*."

He said, "Yes, I know. I read your articles." Maybe this wasn't an accidental meeting? In any case, he didn't say, "Congratulations, you have a great job." But at least he knew I had moved on and very successfully.

The conversation was stilted. It was time to end this. So I said, "I have a meeting to attend and need to head out." I added, "If I or the magazine can help you in any way, just let me know."

What made me say that? Was I identifying with the aggressor? Was it a grand gesture to boast that I have connections? Or maybe that is how abused women respond? "If you want to beat me again, I am OK with that." Mine was a gracious response. It was unwarranted, but I very badly wanted to project that I was in control now. I had moved on.

Later, away from the frenzy of the convention center, I poured myself a glass of wine at home and called Judy. "You won't believe this, but I ran into Pete today."

"What? Did you rail at him? What did you say?

"I really didn't know what to say. It was a shock to see him. He was his usual opaque self. Just standing there, looking blank, like nothing had ever happened. You know what I should have said? Your few minutes of pleasure caused me so much pain. Rolling down that hospital ramp with Ann in my arms is an image I can never erase." I should have painted that scene vividly for him and watched his squirm, but I didn't.

"I wonder why he even bothered to connect," Judy said.

I hung up the receiver, finished my wine, and reflected on that strange encounter. In my mind I untangled and relived each and every stage of the anguish he had caused: first, the sexual assault, and then the degradation of having to confront him on campus. Finally, his unsympathetic, averted eyes in that motel room. When he and his father had walked away from that motel room, I was forced to contend with the detritus of being an unwed mother in a time when society rejected unwed mothers. It was up to me to pick up the pieces

He had no clue or apparent concern for the time I spent suffering in silence though the birth and adoption of his child. This was the most painful chapter of my life so far. And I'd offered to help him?

Maybe I was demonstrating how to be a bigger person. Maybe it was my editor's voice saying, "Keep your enemies close." In any case, I walked away from him and that strange encounter with my dignity and self-respect intact.

Chapter Sixteen

Sexual Freedom

———~~~———

In a few short years, since my campus assault, the birth control pill had dramatically impacting the lives of all women. I welcomed the new attitudes of the sixties. Women were controlling their own bodies, divorce was no longer a scandal, and women were reaching for new careers as professionals. But, sadly, sexual advances in the workplace seemed to accompany these freedoms. Or maybe they were always there.

Starting at age twenty-two, I was ill prepared for the barrage of advances I faced in the office or when traveling for work. Suddenly, I was fair game.

Trying to interview men for articles and having them take me seriously, and not as a sex trinket, was tricky. Arriving to interview the president of an international food company in Boston that had been much in the news, I was hoping for an interesting exchange.

As I strolled into a highly polished staid Boston corporate office, I was in awe of the setting and the views. But while I was shaking the hand of this rather handsome forty-something executive, he gave me an unnerving once-over. What he saw was an attractive twenty-four-year-old that he could corner for the afternoon. I could just hear the gears in his mind changing course as he moved his eyes over me.

Sitting behind his desk and strumming his fingers on a note pad, he said, "It's such a nice day, why don't we go to Marblehead for lunch and take the afternoon off to do the interview?" These were his first words. He wasn't unattractive. He had dazzling blue eyes to match his oxford blue shirt.

"Oh, that won't work for me because I have plans this evening and need to be back in Boston." It was true; I was meeting my sorority sister Janet and her architect boyfriend at his loft on Beacon Hill later.

He reached for his suit jacket and guided me towards the door, promising to have me back in time. With his well-practiced corporate cunning, this executive was simply not taking "no" for an answer. I could see he was more interested in an afternoon affair.

Once in the car, I could not get him into a serious discussion. He kept asking about me and the friends I was meeting later. It was the most laborious ride, even though the splashy New England fall colors along the way were spectacular.

Secretly, I was thrilled the magazine was sending me to the most gorgeous parts of our country for interviews. Yet, in this car, with this man, the experience of trying to get an interview was tedious. He was suave but very aggressive. We lunched at a charming inn, but there was one ploy after another to get me to stay in Marblehead.

"Come on, stay with me longer." He even swerved into a motel driveway to see how I would react.

How many different ways could you say "no" and still be civil? Finally, I said, "My friends will be very concerned. They knew I was meeting with you and will send out alarms if I am not back soon."

The ride home was a hassle. But I persevered, got the story and learned how to be a more forceful woman in the process. What a learning curve.

Another incident of needing to keep a prominent man in check happened on a business trip to New York City. While there, I was doing ground-work for an upcoming press party and planning the final details with the Rainbow Room staff. I was at my professional best arranging these kinds of events.

My plans were almost complete when our vice president called from Chicago to say he was flying to New York that day and wanted to have dinner. I was puzzled. There was no real reason for us to meet, and I wondered how he knew my travel schedule. In the office, he was a dashing figure in pinstriped suits and, often, an ascot. As the chairman of the board's right-hand man, I respected him, but, that evening, I was also onto his "let's have dinner" game plan. As I walked to the Plaza Hotel, I wondered how to deal with this delicate situation. I gathered I was to be his dessert.

We met in the exquisite Walnut Room of the Plaza Hotel, the in place to see and be seen in New York in those days. In this room of shiny wood-paneled walls, elegantly dressed businessmen graced the bar with their feet resting on the brass foot rail revealing highly polished wing tips. The bar was busy serving the glitterati French 75s in thin Champagne flutes. As I sat there waiting for him, I once again realized how far I had traveled from my mill-town upbringing. I knew I would be challenged tonight. I needed to maneuver skillfully through this evening.

As dinner progressed, and as I suspected he would, he started making innuendos about sleeping together. There were only so many ways to brush him off.

The Walnut Room was New York's grand setting for people-watching. He started waving to people across the room and leaned over to say, "You know, my dear, you will have to make love to me now because I will be accused of it anyway. Those are my wife's best friends!" He sat there grinning. Such a bold modus operandi. Such gall on the part of a corporate VP.

I merely said, "Oh, I don't think so. I am not your dessert."

I sat there quietly plotting my next move. He was projecting that he wasn't taking my "no" seriously.

With a saccharine sweet smile, I politely excused myself to the rest room and just kept walking out the side door of the Plaza to a waiting taxi. He would have to have dessert alone.

It was not a very cool move, not very adroit, but it was the best I could think of since "no" wasn't working well. At least he did call the next morning to see if I was OK.

I was too young and inexperienced to know how to cleverly tease him about his effrontery. Speaking truth to power needed more polish, as well as diplomatic language that I did not yet have. I simply took the easy way out and luckily suffered no consequences. I guess it was my dad's advice from my teenage years: "Always have an exit strategy."

Now I could sense sexual advances a mile away. In business, they seemed almost unavoidable. I began to think that office relationships produced unexpected sexual energy. Knowing that actors and actresses working so closely together often became involved, I wasn't surprised to find that was also true in an office. Sexual advances and innuendos were confounding, but I was growing used to brushing them off.

The cigarette advertising slogan of the day, "You've Come a Long Way, Baby," wasn't always so. Those Virginia Slims commercials talked to professional women like me in1968, but women as a whole were not liberated and certainly not immune to sexual harassment.

Men controlled our dress codes and access to their private inner sanctums. In London, I was to meet a publisher for lunch at his club. This sounded exciting and was a first for me. When I arrived in the lobby wearing a tweed pants suit I thought was quite avant-garde for the times, he said, "Oh my dear, I don't think that will do at the club, but we can go elsewhere." I guess we weren't allowed to wear pants just yet.

Although I still carried with me the weight of that sexual assault, I was ready for the warmth of sweet kisses and embraces; I was just not ready to be invaded. I was ready for love again, but would be cautious, very cautious. I had developed my own brand of reserve.

Chapter Seventeen

Shaping a New Life

———～～———

With my career going smoothly, my next priority was to build a new social life. The trendy Near North of Chicago bordering Lake Michigan was the best place for young people in the mid-sixties to meet up. Twenty-somethings could afford to live there in those days, in and around the stately old brownstones lined with leafy tall oaks. Here was easy access to Rush Street, the electric night spot area with lounges and entertainment venues like Mr. Kelly's, where Frank Sinatra or Lenny Bruce enthralled or amused.

Summer days we might check out the Oak Street beach or head west to Wells Street, home of Second City Improv or lunch at casual hangouts like Chances R, where burgers and beer were served with heaping baskets of peanuts in the shell. While finding our table, it was part of the experience to crunch through all the peanut shells underfoot.

In very short time I had collected a group of friends who knew the best ritual gathering sites. My friend Rogner, a sort of big brother and coworker from my earliest magazine days, guided me to all the hot spots. His favorite, Catfish Row, was a small intimate neighborhood bar with a stone floor and a roaring fireplace. "It's the coziest place for a nightcap. Everyone sits by the fire, feet propped up, rehashing their night."

He added, "It's the place for guys to poach their next date."

Rogner was right. On cold nights, drinking rusty nails and relaxing after a dinner date, people gathered there, chatting by the fire, flirting with everyone else. It was like an extension of the fraternity socials where men were sizing up their weekend date.

There were endless bars and restaurants for singles to gather in and around the Near North. The most popular was a lively Irish bar on Division Street, Butch McGuire's, where the faithful gathered. On any Sunday evening, my friends would call to see where we should head out for dinner to find familiar faces.

I was still wary about meeting men in bars, considering my Rathskeller experience. Knowing full well that women alone were vulnerable, I usually went with friends.

One experience cinched for me that the bar scene was not the ideal place to meet men. Even though Butch McGuire's was a happening place at all times, even at brunch, it was still a bar. Stopping there after work one night with a bubbly, attractive coworker, we were soon surrounded by a group of men she knew from none other than Notre Dame. Not knowing her friends, I felt a bit awkward trying to chime in on their usual parochial school stories. I was planning my exit strategy when a good-looking man in a conservative Brooks Brothers style suit approached me. "So, what do you do?" he asked.

He was in town for business, and as we talked, I sized him up as a lonely guy in town just frittering away some time. Eventually he asked about restaurants nearby. His self-assured, cool, and confident style was very much like the men I usually worked with now.

"Why don't we get a hamburger nearby?" he said, and I suggested Chances R, the casual Wells Street spot we all loved.

Over dinner he was forthcoming about his business travels but little else. Still, he seemed normal enough, even if he wasn't very chatty. Eventually he asked, "So, where exactly do you live?"

"Here in the Near North."

"Where, exactly?"

Realizing his intention was to go home with me, I stubbornly deflected all of his questions.

When he became more insistent, I stood up, saying, "I need to get home." But he became even more aggressive. Finally, I had to say, "Hey, you suggested dinner. I am not taking you home."

He turned snarly and said, "Well, what were you doing there, then?"

It's no wonder I have bad feelings about bars and men. Just by being there, we seemed to be fair game. At least I recognized him as a predator and made sure he wasn't following me.

Forgetting the bar scene, I relied more on our spontaneous neighborhood gatherings. My friends, clever at creating pop-up parties in their old brownstones, would stage costume parties, New Year's parties, brunches, etc.

One pop-up happened during a crippling snowstorm. The downtown Chicago traffic was brought to a standstill. The unplowed streets were lined with cars caked in snow like a variety of frosted cupcakes. Lincoln Park instantly became a winter wonderland with cross-country skiers. Everything stopped moving—everything but my friends. They went around ringing doorbells the next morning until they collected a group for brunch at the Pump Room on Astor Street. That was novel. No one had time for brunch during the week, and certainly not at the Pump Room, this posh spot usually reserved for celebrities. But, on that snowy Tuesday morning, our group found our way there.

Between work-related and neighborhood parties, I had acquired a nice set of friends. Many of my friends worked in the test kitchens of the biggest food companies. We were the original "foodies" in Chicago. Our parties became culinary events, like pesto-making parties. Finally, I had an interesting social life alongside a demanding career.

Although my dating opportunities were expanding, I seemed to be checking men off my list as quickly as I met them. One date kept asking me penetrating questions and then leaned over and said something curious. "You don't reveal much of yourself. Why not?"

It was then that I noticed I was avoiding entanglements and attachments. I began hearing similar comments from other dates. "You're really hard to get to know." "What are you really looking for?" "You never seem to be available."

I knew I had reservations when men tried to get more intimate. Maybe I wasn't fully opening up to them because I hadn't met the right one. So far, I hadn't experienced that electric current, like I had with Jim when he came to my door one snowy night. Or, was it me?

I met nice guys, handsome guys, and hip guys, all spinning stories of themselves, pretty much like they do on Facebook today. It was all about them. They talked about what they presently did for fun and who their friends were, without sharing any of their future dreams. Their workdays seemed dull; mine, by comparison, were dazzling. My calendar might include a literary lunch for Nelson Algren or brunch with the chef/owners of the hottest new restaurant. My days were exhilarating, but my evenings seemed to be mundane experiences.

With many dates I would just sit back and watch the night unfold. More often than not, I would look at my watch and think, "This guy is really boring and I have hours to go with him." After a while I decided to be honest and suggest they might like a friend of mine better. Soon, I had developed a new skill as matchmaker. It worked: "I have the perfect person for you." The fun part was being toasted as matchmaker at several of their weddings.

Deep down, I was guarded. The most appealing men, those with thriving careers and exciting lives, were married or unavailable. But with the married ones, I knew I was losing valuable time searching for a real partner while they had nothing to lose.

One available bachelor I did quite like invited me to Maxim's, the hot new discotheque in town. Ed was one date I wanted to know better. He had style and always dressed for work looking like he walked right out of the pages of *Gentleman's Quarterly*. We clandestinely dated within the same company without being discovered for months. He very formally called me "Miss Keller" at work and would drop by my desk for chats. When he suggested a night at Maxim's, it sent me shopping all week for just the right disco dress. I settled on a glitzy dress with fringe and sequins and satin pumps. I loved putting together dating outfits. The anticipation was the fun part.

At the club, I was immediately energized by the flashing strobe lights reflecting onto beaded glass curtains; on the dance floor, bodies twisted and slithered to the music, so close to their partners that the stances were steamy. With arms flailing and lights blinking, it was like watching a sexy, slow-motion tango.

But as we stepped onto the dance, floor I felt my moves were anything but smooth or seductive. I hoped Ed didn't notice my awkward efforts. I suddenly realized how hard it was to physically let go to the music. I couldn't even imitate his waving arms and twisting legs. I was disappointed in my own cumbersome dancing and hoped the flashes from the strobe lights covered my flaws. What had changed in me?

We had a great time that night, but I wondered why I felt so uneasy dancing. I used to love to jitterbug, do the twist, and even engage in ballroom dancing. Now I could sense that my guarded sexuality was even showing on the dance floor. Luckily, Ed didn't seem to notice.

It was pure fun to be with Ed, especially on St. Patrick's Day. I seemed to always attract Irish guys. At one party, someone asked if I was Irish, and hearing no, Ed said, "What? You aren't Irish? I have been taken in!" Spending St.Patrick's Day at his favorite pub, with his spirited friends, was camaraderie at its best. With frothy green beer and too many boilermakers, we both missed our alarm clocks the next morning, and while I was late to work, he was even later.

Ed often had parties at his own row house on Burton Place, this great historic district in the midst of Old Town. Since he was a natural at hosting parties, I asked Ed to help me host my own. I had another reason.

I especially wanted Ed to meet my oldest friend in the world. By a crazy twist of fate, Georgia and I had recently reconnected—it turned out that Jane, the woman who hired me at the magazine, knew Georgia and her husband. Both husbands worked for the same advertising agency.

Just when I most needed a close friend in Chicago, Georgia, my dearest friend from grade school, turned up. We had lost touch around the time Georgia entered her beatnik phase at the University of Pittsburgh. She told me about dressing in a black beret and reading Jack Kerouac in her senior year. This was about the same time I was in my hasty retreat from our hometown. We'd lost track, and this was on purpose on my part.

On my way to meet her, I thought about how the gossips in my hometown loved to shred her and her family.

"Look at you." She was thinner than I remembered, with a fuller head of silky auburn hair, very much like her mother's, and dancing devilish eyes. She had turned into a gorgeous woman in her mid-twenties.

As we sat there exchanging stories and catching up, I didn't dare mention my mysterious past. Observing her dark, heavily mascaraed eyes flashing, I noticed she had the same seductive aura that was there in high school. Looking at me through her new long lashes that seemed to say, "I have a secret," she was the same Georgia I remembered. She had been very busy becoming a mom with a budding career in marketing.

Married now to a successful ad man, her husband Dave salted the conversation with catchy phrases demonstrating a creative flair. I knew Georgia was smart, but she had another talent I never observed before: chutzpah. That is what had helped her to eventually launch her own market research firm in Chicago.

In the decade that followed, Georgia and I frequented the hottest lunch spots and usually settled on the Wrigley Building Restaurant, the mecca for the advertising community. Dressing as stylishly as we dared, Georgia would usually make a dramatic entrance with her eyes flashing, brimming with new secrets to share. We would also chew over the "talk" on Michigan Avenue from bits we gleaned from *Ad Age* (*Advertising Age*) where all the news and gossip for marketing and media groups appeared.

Our favorite upscale lunch spot, Chez Paul, was an elegant restaurant in an old Victorian mansion. In this glamorous setting we couldn't help but compare our simple beginnings to now lunching flamboyantly in Chicago's finest. We prided ourselves in becoming self-assured career women. But, Georgia was not always self-assured. One day over lunch she revealed her Achilles' heel: "Put me in front of a hundred men to give a speech and I flourish with confidence. But, put me in a small room of women and I wilt." That comment told much about the damage our small-town gossips had inflicted on her because of her mother's perceived bad reputation as a divorcee. Listening that day made me grateful my parents had the foresight to keep me under the radar of our town's whisperers. As yet, I had not breathed a word to her about my Achilles' heel.

She loved to probe for details about who I was dating. Thinking she should see for herself, I decided to invite Georgia and her husband to my next cocktail party so she could meet Ed and my new collection of friends. That night they circulated through my crowded noisy party, and when they were leaving I asked, "So what do you think of Ed and my sundry friends? I want the real truth."

Her husband, used to a zany mix of people in his agency, very sincerely said, "They're all nice people, but they seem to be cut from the same cookie-cutter mold."

This was something I had been feeling, too. There was little diversity in my group, while the times around me were changing so dramatically. My friends were comfortable yet conventional, very buttoned down, but they weren't expanding themselves in these changing times. There were no love beads, big hairstyles, or bell bottoms. They were the khaki pants, navy blazer, and penny loafers crowd, just like in college. I wasn't stretching myself. I needed more diverse friends.

Just when I was thinking I needed to widen my circle, an offbeat guy kept coming into my office at work. He had a fresh, crewcut "boy next door" look and a passion for Chicago blues. Although I was not physically attracted to him and I did not share his other interest in stock car racing, I found his music interest compelling. "Come out with me one night to hear the real Chicago blues," he said. I was warming to the idea.

One fall evening he took me after dinner to the famous open-air Maxwell Street Market. We walked among the eclectic merchants setting out mainly handmade wares for the next day. It was cold enough for open-air firepits. The smoky aromas of savory Polish sausages and grilled onions filled the air. We sat sipping coffee and waiting for the real musicians of Chicago blues to show up. Muddy Waters, Little Walter, and Bo Diddley were known to play at Maxwell Street after hours. We were ready to wait it out.

We kept looking around for Muddy while other Black musicians soulfully blasted out their blues. It was a magic moment sitting there in the night air. This was a whole new dimension for me, trusting someone to take me into uncharted waters like midnight at Maxwell Street. As we hovered over open firepits rubbing hands to keep warm, the red coals seemed to be dancing to the beat of the blues. Tantalizing aromas were rising in the night air.

That was an authentic Chicago experience, a magical moment as we sat there feeling the amplified sounds of guitars and watching the vendors spread out bolts of fabric, old tires, housewares, sofas, fur coats, and anything they could sell. It was a special night listening to those distinctive blues chords in the crisp night air—the same sounds that had been spreading through the streets and bars in Chicago.

My date was an unusual guy, not from the cookie-cutter mold for sure, and I loved that he sought new experiences. Looking up at the sky we saw the first crack of morning light. Unfortunately, the only sparks flying for me that night were the sparks from the fire.

Chapter Eighteen

My Mad Men Years

Again, itching to change jobs, I was looking beyond the staid corporate scene—pin-striped suits, wing tips and all. I was ready for another challenge. There was an electric energy emanating from the advertising agencies on Michigan Avenue, and I wanted to understand what the excitement was about. That world of advertising was tempting me.

At noontime convertibles would drive down Michigan Avenue with animated women sitting on top brandishing products and yelling out ad slogans like, "Flick Your Bic," to highlight the Bic cigarette lighter. Samples of cigarettes were also thrown from cars to the crowds bustling to lunch. Noontime on Michigan Avenue could be as colorful as the agencies testing their products and slogans. Handheld signs fresh from the creative departments in floors above Michigan Avenue tested market acceptance. This seemed way more exciting than test kitchens.

That vitality of the advertising community was calling to me. There were so few women in the advertising ranks, but I was burning to give it a try. I set out to roll the dice and see if I could join a creative team.

The agency promoting the lively slogan, "You've Come a Long Way, Baby" for Virginia Slims cigarettes, was right down the street at Leo Burnett. I started poking around the agency to see if they would hire me.

Walking right up to their reception area at Leo Burnett, one of the largest agencies, I asked who would accept a resume. Following all the right steps, I finally landed an interview with the head of the office.

When I sat down in front of him, he first looked at his watch (not a good sign) and then said, "You know we have our own test kitchen, so what do you think you can offer that isn't already being done at Leo Burnett?"

He missed the point. I had applied as a copywriter— I gathered that my magazine articles, food photography and writing samples weren't of interest. I didn't have a good response to his question. I sensed the interview was a flop and felt defeated.

But I wasn't about to give up. Advertising was coming of age in the sixties, and it was hard not to notice the creativity exploding in print and lively commercials. The "Think Small" campaign for the Volkswagen Beetle was brilliant. The brevity and wit of that offered a stark contrast with wordy ads for the big-finned muscular cars of the fifties. Pepsi had successful two-word campaigns as well: "Think Young" and the "Pepsi Generation." Would I ever be able to condense my verbose editorial style into two short words?

Not hearing back from Leo Burnett, I dusted myself off and tried another, even bigger agency. Advertising agencies had a very different environment from the polished corporate scene I was used to—the decor screamed with bold colors; men wore crazy hairstyles, and women wore casual short skirts and tall boots. From what I could gather from the animated behavior coming and going in the reception area, these were spirited places to work. Agencies were more in tune with the lively times.

My next interview went better. Landing a job as copywriter in the creative department at J. Walter Thompson, I would be focusing on their restaurant and food service accounts. It was the largest advertising agency in the country at the time, and I was ecstatic. It was a whole new twist for my career path.

Wanting to first travel and take a break, I negotiated a month-long vacation before starting at the agency. The year before, 1967—the "Summer of Love"— I'd gone to England to check out the theme I had seen on banners around town, *The British Are Coming.* England had suddenly become the center of music and fashion; I wanted to go back to London and other parts of Europe. This just might help me transition into this hip new world of advertising. Plus, I had several names of people to help pave my way once there.

Traveling alone was challenging, but it produced some surprising changes in me. The experience allowed me to be more outgoing with strangers. In Geneva, Swiss restaurants with long, comfortable counters serving food were inviting. I grew comfortable initiating conversations. In one case, a handsome French man who was in Geneva attending a medical meeting shared his recipe for Niçoise salad. It was easy for me to talk food wherever I was. He ended up guiding me on a sightseeing tour that afternoon.

My audience was no longer just twenty-somethings. One evening while dining by myself I noticed an older, obviously intoxicated American woman in the hotel dining room. She was flailing around in her seat while chastising the waiter. Knocking over her martini, she slurred, "This steak is nothing like ours in Texas. At least we know our beef." I gathered from her rantings that they owned a cattle ranch.

Her behavior was embarrassing, especially because she was portraying an insensitive, ugly image of Americans. With raised eyebrows and heads turning to watch, her younger companion threw down his napkin and left the table in a huff saying, "Mother, you disgust me."

I felt a need to intercede. This drunk American was causing quite a stir. I went over to her table and asked, "Are you staying in the hotel?" I could see her keys on the table.

"Well, so am I. I am from Chicago. Why don't you let me walk you up to your room?"

She slumped in her chair like a scolded child and said, "OK, sweetheart."

Once at her door, I gently knocked and her son answered. Seeing his mother in tow, he allowed his distraught face to slowly relax.

"Thank you. I just can't stand when Mother starts drinking too much. That was very kind of you."

In Madrid I learned to polish my skills in diplomacy. Taking a bus tour to a bullfight one afternoon, I befriended a soft-spoken American lawyer. He asked if we could have dinner later. I said yes, but by now knew to add, "… But with no strings attached."

Over dinner he entertained me with his storytelling. His life was not nearly as quiet as his somber demeanor suggested. He regaled me with his stories and then hinted at sharing his bed, as I suspected he would again. I didn't like him well enough for that, but had finally figured out how to be politely tactful: "This has been lovely, but I am not up for an entanglement."

I learned to say "no" and "police" in every language. A woman traveling by herself was always a target, and especially so in Italy. Staying in a variety of pensions, small hotels, and meager bed-and-breakfast inns, I found that the owners, even with their wives present, were abashedly forward, pinching or touching inappropriately. Yet, the pensions were colorful experiences. Pans rattled and insults poured from the kitchen. In the dining room, I would endure polite but teasing advances from the proprietor while his wife served the cappuccino. Once they were back in the kitchen, the salty curses continued. After all of this local color, shabby rooms and all, I was ready to splurge on a luxury hotel.

The Splendido in Portofino fit the bill. But it was far from the town center, and the train didn't go the whole way, so I ended up on a protracted taxi ride from the station. I kept asking the driver in Italian, "How much farther?"

Never understanding his answer in Italian, I was a wreck. Why was it taking so long? Had he misunderstood my directions? When we finally arrived, I was in a highly agitated state and ran to the front desk to confirm I was booked there, then volunteered, "I am a single woman traveling alone and that was one long, stressful cab ride."

Later that night, there was a knock on my door. That same manager had his foot wedged in the door. The single woman traveling alone bit hadn't worked out too well.

The manager said, "I thought madame might need something tonight."

"No, I do not," I sternly said, but he would not leave. Who was I supposed to call, the front desk?

Realizing that, conveniently, no one else was booked at my end of the floor, I went to the phone and said I was calling the "polizia." That he understood.

London would be a welcome change—no language barriers and no pinching men. My first destination was to Soho to visit the swinging Carnaby Street. This three-block alley I had read about was home of the hottest new fashion trends in England. Apparently, Jimi Hendrix, Pete Townshend, the Beatles, and the Rolling Stones all frequented boutiques like the Tom Cat, Lady Jane, and Lord Jim. These shops were on my list, and I wanted to see what the excitement was all about.

Swathes of colored banners lined Carnaby Street. There was almost a frenzy of shopping on the street for "mod" outfits, short dresses, miniskirts, belts, and boots. Like in Filene's Basement in Boston, people were trying clothes on in the aisles or in back communal rooms. Here they were changing right out in the store front, causing traffic to slow down for the show. It was chaos. Designers were patching together the first ensembles of the season. I was brave enough to buy my first white minidress with black geometric patterns on top.

Before leaving Chicago, a few of my business friends, with branch offices in London, set me up with contacts. One was the head of Playboy International. I was little trepidatious about meeting this one. But, a firm date had been set, and I was to call him on my arrival in London.

When I returned to my hotel, with my shopping bags from Carnaby Street, I learned that he had left me a message for me to call. I could still back out. But I had this fun new minidress to wear now. When I called him, confirming I was free that night, he said, "I will send my driver to pick you up." He was so easy to talk with, asking if I was tired and ready for a quiet dinner. "There is a small dinner party tonight at my townhouse." A driver? At his townhouse? This was impressive. Fun thoughts were swirling around Should I wear the new minidress? I was still a traditional girl at heart, wearing suits and heels to work and sometimes hat and gloves. If I wasn't bold enough to wear that minidress in London, then where?

Mounting the steps to his townhouse in my black-and-white, geometric-patterned short dress and black patent pumps, I was ready. What I wasn't prepared for was the jet-set lifestyle that unfolded in front of me that night.

His driver took me in to meet Victor where he was unpacking his suitcase from a trip. I was not used to meeting men in their bedrooms, but he politely jabbered away, giving me sideways glances over his glasses. I could sense a strong personality, but with an urbane, not flashy, demeanor. He set me at ease by asking about myself and talking about his Chicago years.

A cute terrier jumped on his bed. "What's his name?"

"Eros."

"That's a strange name for dog." Another of my *Alice in Wonderland*, naive comments that seemed to drop out without thinking.

Instead of responding, he said, "Let's go meet the guests."

His guests included a hip disc jockey from Paris, an art collector, Sammy Davis, Jr., and a few women somehow connected with Playboy ... maybe former bunnies? Around the table the conversation was fresh. The disc jockey was highly animated, and Sammy was, as expected, entertaining.

Sitting next to him, I was surprised how open he was with his feelings.

"I will never fall in love again. It's just too painful," he said. He had been married to the Swedish actress May Britt. You could feel from him the torture of losing a love.

What I found inside this Playboy milieu were very colorful guests willing to share their inner feelings openly. I sat there contrasting this scene to my very own provincial upbringing where you never mentioned personal feelings, especially at the dinner table.

After dinner, we all went to a private London club where Rex Harrison and other recognizable faces were dancing. My miniskirt matched the scene perfectly. With Marvin Gaye's "I Heard It Through the Grapevine" playing and strobe lights flashing, I danced with much more flair. Remembering how awkward I felt dancing at Maxim's, I thought to myself, "I am loosening up. Is it London or me?" There was a warm feeling brewing between Victor and me. I looked around at all the glitterati I was suddenly a part of and wondered if it was real or I was just dreaming.

Looking over his shoulder, he said, "I want you to meet someone. A troubled woman. … I'll explain later."

"Hey, Christine. How are you doin'? This is my friend from Chicago."

Christine turned around and I saw a woman stylishly dressed but with deeply sad eyes. It was Christine Keeler, the woman involved in the highly publicized British political scandal, the profumo affair. John Profumo had been Secretary of State for War under Prime Minister Harold MacMillan, and his affair with Christine, just nineteen at the time, had led not only to his dismissal but the resignation of MacMillan. It was a huge scandal. I knew her name and was surprised at what a simple girl she appeared to be to capture such headlines and topple a head of state.

It was an exotic evening, to say the least. Victor topped it off by asking if I would stay and travel with him through Italy. What an invitation—spending time on the Riviera with this suave guy! His lifestyle was flamboyant and he seemed to sincerely want my companionship. I knew it would be quite the adventure for me. When would I get a chance to peek into the lives of the European jet set again?

But my conventional side drew me back to Earth. I'd been working hard to build a successful career, scheming hard to secure my advertising job. I wasn't sure I should jeopardize the stable life I had built for an unknown venture. Respectability was still part of my drive, and I thought I just might be throwing it away. Yet maybe this was just what I needed, to break free for a while. It was not the first time my conservative self and my adventurous self were in conflict, tugging at me in these liberating times. What if I called the agency to say I couldn't start on the target date?

In the end, I decided not to place myself in a state of uncertainty with someone I barely knew, after all I had been through. "I would love that, Victor, but I just can't. I need to get back to Chicago." I saw that my travels had given me a new self-realization and conviction.

When I returned to Chicago and walked by the Playboy Mansion on State Street, I was intrigued to think I had peered into that inner sanctum in London. I wondered what went on behind those walls in the Chicago mansion; I knew of the scantily clothed women in bunny outfits serving drinks, but I also knew Hugh Hefner was known for advocating sexual liberation. I factored in the Playboy sexist image, but his Chicago mansion, ironically, was a place for women's rights activism. Fundraising events at that Mansion promoted some of the early feminist organizations.

In the early seventies, Hefner even provided the seed money for the American Civil Liberties Union's Women's Rights Project, that, I later learned, was co-founded by the then little-known lawyer, Ruth Bader Ginsburg. And, Playboy funded the rape kit project so that police could finally start treating sexual assault as a crime. That was a huge step forward for women who had been raped.

I applauded anyone, including Hugh Hefner, who stood up for women. After the suffering I endured in silence, my limited choices, and the shame surrounding it all, standing up for women's rights put a whole new meaning to sexual liberation. I could put up with the scantily clothed bunnies because Hugh Hefner supported women. My views were being stretched again.

That month in Europe, mixing it up with different kinds of people—fishermen, shopkeepers, artists or traveling families—over crusty loaves and carafes of wine, I had broadened my ability to engage strangers. Most especially, I was becoming adroit at maneuvering among men. I could easily talk with them or flirt with them or keep them at a distance, depending on my instincts. Expanding way beyond the twenty-somethings of my "in group" in the Near North, I could appreciate and enjoy people not "just like me." What had taken me so long?

Refreshed from this journey, I was ready to tackle this new world of advertising. The AMC series *Mad Men* painted those times with crystal clarity. The offices were filled with smoke, alcohol, and lecherous men. Trying to fit in, I observed that being clever won points. Boring straight talk did not. "Catching my chooch to the burbs" was just one way for a creative director to say goodnight as he left the office.

And, yes, my own creative director was just as handsome as Don Draper, except he wore cowboy boots with a suit jacket and jeans. He was the exact image of the Marlboro Man, a masculine, handsome outdoor type. What a trendsetter. When he stomped into a client meeting, his commanding presence was felt.

Like Draper, he was just as fast on his feet, coming up with clever campaigns on the spot. (When I later watched *Mad*

Men, I was convinced that Don was based on that very same creative director.)

Coming up short on my copy deadline for Quaker Oats, I was called into his office so he could see what I had. A bit nervous that I was not going to knock his socks off, I kept starring at his cowboy boots and wondering if he had a pair of wing tips in his drawer for client meetings.

As he read my slogans for instant cereal packets, I could see his forehead wrinkle as dismay started spreading across his face. Trying to react first, I quickly offered, "I have trouble putting together short slogans. I'm used to writing flowery food copy."

"Well, this isn't a goddamned magazine; say it in fewer words." Even back then, a two-word slogan was worth reaching for. Frustrated, he walked to his bookshelf, pulled out a book, and more or less threw it at me. *The Art of Readable Writing* is still on my bookshelf today.

"This will help." Almost apologetically he said, "Look, it isn't that hard. Just try to condense your words. Think product virtues. Think this way: Good things come in small packages. How hard is that?"

I stood there melting into the floor, blinking back tears. This was the second boss to make me tear up. But I respected them for the lessons they were pounding into me. They cared enough to make time to teach. Learning to take criticism is also an art, so l bounced up to look over his shoulder at the book. In spite of the reprimand, I respected him as a leader. He was the giant guiding light at that agency. I just felt honored for the attention.

Best of all, going to work was an adventure once again. Being around all this creative energy was stimulating. The crazies on the creative side, with their bushy big Afros and large personalities, resided alongside the buttoned-down account men. There was an interesting synergy watching them work together. It was such fun to be part of that atmosphere, especially when celebrations were under way around winning a new account. It was the true *Mad Men* scene, with cigarette smoke swirling and alcohol flowing. I was almost sad when Saturday rolled around to end the creative spunk in the office. It was a great time to be in the ad business. I was glad I hadn't chosen the Riviera.

Chapter Nineteen

Kismet

—◦◦◦—

My traumatic early experiences as a college senior were being buried even deeper. Dating often in those liberated sixties, I was very aware of my intimacy issues with men, all the time wondering if I could ever trust again—until one date where food and adventure unlocked my heart.

The ad agency where I now worked was located in the newest and most dramatic skyscraper in Chicago. Just looking up at the architecture of the John Hancock Building was a thrill. As I walked down the hall in the creative department, each cubicle seemed to scream for attention. Hand-lettered slogans laced with floral designs and wavy images decorating the walls amplified the spirit of the sixties. My new job in advertising pumped up my pulse.

Newly won accounts were celebrated with lavish cocktail parties dripping with all the excesses this *Mad Men*-era group could muster. These alcohol-drenched gatherings were much crazier than the ones in the corporate life I had left behind. And, they were different, too, from the antics at the publishing house, but I was bent on stretching myself into this new experience. As usual, I kept my antennae turned up. There were plenty of lechers around, bringing me drinks. I was wary.

Spontaneously, one fall afternoon, I decided to head across Michigan Avenue to an Advertising Club luncheon to hone my networking skills. Before the program began, an intriguing man, a bit older, in a well-tailored suit and a carefully styled beard came over to my table. I finally remembered him well from the year before, when I had introduced him as the speaker at my own professional meeting.

How could I forget him? Sitting with him at the speaker's table that night, his vitality had captured my attention completely. He vividly painted his impressions of the youth movement. Those vital young people were thinking out of the box, he had said. He offered tales of his own college-age kids—their campus sit-ins, taking them to rock concerts, and weaving in his own thoughts on the counterculture and music of the day. I could feel his zeal for the times. He seemed to have more depth than the men I usually dated. Here was a man so involved in the world around him. I was fascinated listening to him and wished the people in the audience could disappear so we could just keep talking.

When it was time to introduce him as speaker, I had read his background, including the fact that he was a "father of four." After his speech that night he leaned over to ask, "Would you care to stop for a drink nearby?" As much as I wanted to, I remembered his "father of four" bio; I didn't want to get entangled with a married man.

I offered as an excuse. "That would be nice, but I need to finish a project tonight."

The next morning, I felt sorry for that quick response. Why didn't I at least go for that drink? So, I called him to thank him for speaking, hoping he would ask me out again. But, that was a year ago, and he had never called again.

That afternoon when he came to my table, after some casual conversation, he finally asked, "Meredith, are up for an adventure? Would you like to go on a yacht race Saturday?"

I already knew a bit about him, that he headed a successful marketing and design firm, yet it stayed with me that he had talked so fondly about each of his kids. I felt he must be a devoted dad. At least now we could finish that conversation.

My snap decision, "Yes," was because I would now have the chance to find out his marital status and more about this compelling person called Bill. He was forty-five, much older than I was, and a father of four. What was I thinking? My summer travels, though, had given me broadened views about people. And, he was different."

Sailing would be a new adventure. In the past five years I had been gazing at Chicago's impressive lakefront with those brightly colored sails I had never once stepped aboard a sailboat. When I arrived that Saturday in open-toed sandals— rather than topsiders, the usual deck shoes—and a short culotte outfit, he must have known it was my maiden voyage. I knew as soon as I stepped on deck no one would mistake me for a seasoned sailor. I didn't even bring a thick-knit sweater for the cool lake breezes. But, still, Bill beamed as I boarded amid a flurry of activity, sails being set, the crew checking halyards, someone stowing beer. Through all the clanking and clamor, brief introductions were shouted to his crew, who were mostly my age.

"Sit there, out of harm's way," he said, and before I knew it we were suddenly off to a new adventure.

Sitting in the cockpit, I was tense with all the chaos of the starting maneuvers. Once underway, the boat made a dash to the starting line, slicing through the water and heeling just a bit. So far, so good. One of the crew, holding a stopwatch,

called out minutes and finally seconds to the start. Then I heard the crack of the starting gun as we crossed the invisible starting line. The chaos began when boats suddenly changed course. When boats crossed our bow the crew began shouting "Starboard!" or "Right of way." It looked like imminent collision everywhere I looked. All the frenzied activity had me on edge.

Bill seemed a competent skipper, especially when other boats were converging on the mark at the same time. This was more excitement than I anticipated—it was like a game of chicken, with boats falling away or holding course.

When the boat heeled over, my body stiffened. I was terrified but tried not to show it. Then, as we headed for the next mark, boats were lined up in a row, heeled way over with their sails practically dipping in the water. The crew scrambled to the high side. What a thrilling sight. My knuckles were white from holding on to the gunwales. Rounding the mark, you heard the headsail beating wildly as it was brought down. Then, there was a popping sound as huge spinnakers filled with air and snapped into place. It was a gorgeous sight to see all these colorful sails ballooning out as each boat rounded the mark. I had seen these billowing spinnakers from shore but being on board was an entirely new thrill.

Once the tensions of the race were over, the wind- and sunburned crew sailed back towards the harbor. Popping open cold beer, they were relaxing and reliving each tactical decision with relish. Bill seemed exhilarated, and I enjoyed their banter. It was all new and exciting.

After the boat was secured and back in the harbor, Bill said, "What did you think of the race, Meredith?

"It was such a big rush. Each mark you rounded had my heart in my mouth."

"Were you ever in a race before?" He sipped his beer and watched my reaction.

"No, but It was exciting."

I sensed that racing was the weekend passion for his crew as well, who, I learned, were mostly commodity traders. Their competitive spirit ran high as they jabbed and joked with each other after the race.

"So, winning is everything?" I asked.

"No. It's how you sail the race that counts."

I remembered during the race Bill checking with the crew for their input on wind speeds and direction; the teamwork was amazing to watch.

After the race. he invited the crew up to his apartment overlooking the harbor for gin and tonics. Hopefully, now I could get his real story—married, divorced, or just a playboy?

Stepping out on the balcony of his apartment, he pointed out how we could look down and spot his yacht in the harbor.

"So, have you lived here long?

I saw him stiffen slightly as he mentioned being divorced and only having moved recently to this high-rise overlooking Belmont Harbor.

"I can even walk across the street and jump that fence to get to my boat," he said, gesturing towards the harbor. I could read his love of sailing. Even though I didn't yet know his whole story, I was immediately comfortable with him, and totally ready for the next step when he asked, "Would you like to have dinner with me?"

As his crew was taking off, he offered that we could have dinner in the neighborhood, and he began naming the restaurants.

"Or, I could cook dinner for you."

That was an impressive offer.

"I can make a Hungarian dish from my family traditions—chicken paprikash." He looked Hungarian, I thought.

"OK. That sounds interesting."

We went into the kitchen, and he began gathering ingredients from the refrigerator. He pulled out a bottle of Champagne and filled our glasses while explaining in great detail his process for chopping up a whole chicken while setting aside pieces of fat.

"This is an important next step, rendering the chicken fat. Some of the skin turns into crisp, edible bits."

He called them "grommels". He popped the pieces of fat into the skillet. It took a while to render the fat. When the pieces of skin turned a rich, dark color, he took them out to drain and salt them.

"Here, try this. My mother would give us these as a treat while she was cooking."

More Champagne revealed that he had been raised in an orphan home since age twelve, and those fond memories of his mother cooking paprikash in younger years were very special to him. While chopping onions and cubing potatoes and sprinkling them liberally with a dusting of paprika, salt, and pepper, bits and pieces of his life bubbled out just like the Champagne.

Into the pan of rendered chicken fat went the chopped onions to "sauté until golden. That rendered fat is called *schmaltz;* you can buy it in grocery stores now, but my grandma and mom made their own. We would even spread it on Jewish rye toast instead of butter and rub it with garlic. We were very poor during those Depression years, and it was a treat."

He told me that his father had died when he was twelve, leaving his mom with three young boys to raise and no means to support them. "We three went into a Jewish orphan home in Cleveland, and I stayed there through high school, letting the younger two eventually go home with Mom when she could manage them."

He added, "Paprikash is the only dish I know how to make. In the orphan home we had tasks like peeling potatoes … but never cooking." Now as he added the chicken, his kitchen was becoming warmly scented with a spicy blend of sautéing onion and the pungent jab of paprika. There were other questions I wanted to ask about his later life, but didn't want to interrupt the flow. I was warmed by the Champagne but even more so by the way he was tiptoeing into my heart. I wanted to ask about his later life, but I didn't want to ruin his culinary show. Not yet.

"You cover the pot and let the chicken pieces cook a bit before adding the potatoes."

Here was someone revealing himself just as slowly and as carefully as the dish he was preparing for me, thoughtfully seasoning his story and the chicken at the same time. What a great way into my heart, storytelling through food and wine.

He wrinkled his brow and inquisitively asked, "You seem self-assured and comfortable with yourself. Am I right? So many of the women I've met recently are neurotic, and you're not."

Knowing he held psychology degrees his questions were my first insight into how direct he would be. How was I to answer that question simply?

"My career gives me confidence, I guess. I know who I am. In that respect, I do feel comfortable in my skin. Besides, I can switch jobs whenever I feel like it. Right now I'm loving advertising, but that could change."

Bill then added the potatoes and started mixing a salad. I pitched in to make the dressing ... we were working as a team.

Lighting candles and opening more Champagne, he filled our glasses and made a simple toast. "*Salud, pesetas, amor, y el tiempo para gastarlas* ... or: to health, wealth, love, and the time to enjoy them." He told me he'd picked the toast up in Mexico after the war. He said he'd gone there to study Spanish, and he proceeded to tell me all about his life there after the war.

I felt honored—someone cooking for me, connecting with me, and toasting me on a first date.

Slowly he was peeling away bits and pieces of his life. This included telling me about another woman he lived with after his divorce. I wondered if it was over. But I was warmed by how willing he was to unveil his life so soon, and since he talked openly about losing his family through divorce, I was aware of the depths of his feelings.

After a blistering divorce, Bill had been going through a dating list donated by a seasoned bachelor friend. He was finding the dates amusing but frustrating. "Most of them were neurotic. One recent divorcee was still so wounded she started crying uncontrollably when talking about her husband. Then, she ran out of the apartment," he said.

After hearing his stories, I brought up my travels. As we talked, I felt the same as I had the night I met him a year earlier at the speaker's table. Here was a smart man of so many interests and passions, a real Renaissance man. I felt so comfortable at that moment and wanted to know him better.

He must have had similar thoughts about me, because he leaned over, put his hand on mine and asked very simply, "Would you like to stay the night?"

Why could I relate so quickly to him and not to men closer to my age? How had he broken down the barriers that allowed me to accept him, a divorced man with four children, and immediately trust him so completely?

Trust was the key to my heart and I was surprised at my own quick response. There was a comfort level with him that I had not felt with other men. After my early sexual assault, trust was a key ingredient. Asking me that first night gently *if* I would like to stay over was the first sign. It wasn't a sales pitch or coercion. It was a sweet sincere approach that I could have easily declined. It wasn't an ultimatum. He was asking for consent.

The next day Bill asked if we could get dinner somewhere in my neighborhood. I wondered where to take him and thought of my usual Near North Sunday spots. When he showed up in shorts and dark oxfords with dark socks, not the cool Near North look of casual loafers with no sox, it was my first hint he was a non-conformist.

On our second date, instead of flowers he brought me a bag of books. Again, not the usual gesture. I was amused as he pulled out each one, telling me his reasons for choosing it.

"I would like to share these with you, and maybe we can discuss them together." That was novel and even compelling. No one else cared what I was reading. Was I going to be quizzed on these?

Over the few weeks that followed, he showered me with attention in ways no other man had. But the most meaningful kind of attention was when he called early one morning in the middle of a thunderstorm to see if he could drive me to work. He knew that sheeting rain would soak me to the bone before I got there. That was remarkable to me. He had shown his protective side.

On weekends, as we walked through his neighborhood, we were in and out of record shops looking for the latest albums of the day. Bill loved the intense lyrics of the Doors and the Rolling Stones. I was more in tune with the serenity of "The Sound of Silence" by Simon and Garfunkel, including their lyrics, "The vision that was planted in my brain still remains, within the sound of silence." I was beginning to notice that we were quite different people. Were we on a collision course?

After inviting him for dinner one night, I went about staging a quiet, romantic dinner with candlelight. I was on a mission to find logs for the fireplace and just the right bittersweet chocolate for my mousse. It was a crisp October evening with fall aromas filling the night air. I was excited for the evening.

My new apartment was in a brownstone with natural charm, but I added even more that night, with pumpkins and some straw flowers he'd bought me on a recent walk. We were just about to have the chocolate mousse when the romantic mood was sharply interrupted by the sound of shattering glass, thwacking sounds on metal and screeches from what appeared to be an angry mob outside. We ran to the balcony of my Dearborn apartment and saw "The Days of Rage" in action. Bill knew right away what was happening, but I was in shock.

That night, October 8, 1969, there was a mass action in Lincoln Park just a block away from my apartment. Mainly, it was members of the newly formed, more militant faction of the SDS (Students for a Democratic Society), called the Weathermen. The gathering in the park and the demonstration that night were meant to jolt people out of complacency about the ongoing Vietnam War. They were supposedly heading down to the Loop to demonstrate in front of the hotel where Judge Julius Hoffman was staying. He was presiding over the ongoing trial of those accused of causing the protests at the Democratic Convention in 1968. But instead, the rally had ended in chaos. The mob made its way down Dearborn, smashing car windows and denting cars, and headed towards the Loop. Later, there were arrests and shootings.

Looking out my window at the destruction, I was revulsed.

Then, I saw Bill, looking on from my balcony, smiling at the protestors. Baffled, I said, "Why do you think this is OK?"

"There is a backdrop to their actions. This has been simmering for some time. Remember the protests outside the Democratic Convention last year and the police clubbing the protestors?"

We know all eyes were on the outbursts from of the convention, I said.

"Well, the Chicago Eight, these young men who were trying to end the war, were charged with conspiring to incite those riots," Bill said. "Their trial is still underway. No one is listening to these frustrated kids, and all they want is to end the war. They are beyond frustrated."

I was still stunned by those rampaging right down my street. But as shocked as I was by the destruction, Bill interpreted their action in a different way. "It was their utter frustration," he said, but I was puzzled by his reaction and political views.

As we talked late into the night, I learned he had so many passions and interests beyond work. He was an activist, going to Washington with a group of business leaders to call on Congress to end the war. Nothing they did seemed to be working, either. He, too, was frustrated. I was observing a new side of him that scared me a bit, the activist side. I was not that political.

Yet, Bill was so solicitous of me that he was easily becoming my constant companion. When he suggested a weekend together in New York City, I hesitated, feeling it could be awkward spending that much time together. But, I needn't have worried. Being with him was much like that first sailing race, a new experience yet purposeful, thoughtful, and exciting. Walking the city from the Village to Central Park was magical. He even offered to go to church with me Sunday. This was refreshing. I didn't have to conform to his religion? When it came time to board our plane, I didn't want the weekend to end.

Slowly, I was becoming attached to someone again. Was this the real thing? I always heard it wasn't a question of if you could live with someone but if you could live without them. We were not the least bit alike. He was a Type A personality, and I was low-key. He was Jewish; I was Episcopalian. He was sixteen years older!

Just before I met Bill, I had been seeing a single guy my age, an account man from the ad agency. Several weeks earlier, he had invited me to a formal charity ball. It was on my calendar for the next weekend, and when I came clean about it, Bill seemed dejected, even though I assured him this guy was not a serious man in my life.

The Friday before the ball, he asked me to meet him in a park. I had a lunch to go to, but he wanted to see me before my lunch. Walking there, I kept wondering why the spontaneous meeting. There was such insistence in his voice.

When I arrived at the park, he was already there, arms folded and looking very pensive. He had me sit down on a park bench, took my hands, and gazed intensely at me.

He simply said, "You must know I am very much in love with you. I think of you all day and want to have you in my life always. I want to marry you."

That was a stunning surprise. It was not like Jim saying he wanted me to be the mother of his children. Bill simply wanted me to share his life.

This special announcement included no pomp, no flourishes, no flowers, no ring ... but I was taken by his forthright manner and transparent sincerity. It was his trademark, I later learned—he was never one to be bashful about expressing his feelings. A wave of warmth spread over me as I squeezed his hand and gently kissed him, but I did not say yes. The scent of his aftershave stayed with me all weekend. That proposal was strategically timed to coincide with my upcoming date. I guessed he thought my date was a serious contender.

During my travels the previous summer, a respected English publisher had suggested different career opportunities for me there in London. "Don't go back to the States, get married, and live in the suburbs. Come to London. It is exciting right now." His words kept drifting in and out of my thoughts.

That night at the formal ball, my date kept name-dropping at the table and bragging about his new assignments in Europe, repeating them as if no one had heard him the first time. During the evening, I kept thinking of Bill, smiling to myself, knowing I had found someone who was very sure of himself and filled with challenging adventures of his own. He was offering me his hand to join the next phase of his life.

Bill and I were married two-and-a-half months later at the end of 1969. I guess he did not want me to get away. And, I hadn't even had time to read his bag of books!

We eventually did move to the suburbs, and I never stopped for a minute to think what might be ahead for me as a new wife and stepmother.

Chapter Twenty

Adapting ... to the Seventies

Adaptation was required for each step of my way since 1962. Along with my marriage to Bill came two children in college and two in high school. Campus protests, shootings at Kent State, the Pentagon Papers, and eventually the Watergate scandal were all mixed into the social fabric of the seventies. Bill was increasingly concerned about the social unrest. Meanwhile, I was busy adjusting to my new role as a wife and learning what it was like to be a stepmom. Although they did not live with us, getting used to a ready-made family who seemed to think of me as the "other" (not the "mother") brought a few hiccups.

They were fully formed teenagers and young adults off at boarding schools or colleges. I wasn't their mother, the all-important nurturing figure, but more like another of Dad's girlfriends. Maybe because our marriage was so quick, they had not quite adjusted yet. One way to put it is I didn't feel I had any standing within their family to begin with. Not yet.

His divorce, although several years before, left his wife filled with rancor she would continue to inflict over the years. This wasn't unusual in divorces, but I was not prepared for the drama ahead.

That first Christmas was puzzling. His former wife threw the kids out of her house Christmas Eve because they lingered too long with us over dinner. This was hard for all of us to process, and soon the brood of backpacking kids was back in our apartment feeling hurt. I wondered what my role should be in this drama.

Doing what I know to do best and what centered me the most, I started baking: all kinds of Christmas cookies, including labor-intensive deep-fried Swedish rosettes, hand-pressed shortbread cookies, and the buttery Russian tea cookies. Conscious of creating new traditions and trying to blend in their family traditions, I added potato latkes to the menu of roast beef with Yorkshire pudding. I was hoping to win my way into their hearts through food, as Bill had done for me. However, I soon found that there was a learning curve. His kids, like others of the new "Me" generation, a mix of hedonism and idealism, were more bent on focusing on health foods. Some were even vegetarians, so the roast beef would not be a hit. They weren't strict vegans yet, just leaning in that direction. There went traditional Christmas menus as I'd known them.

This group had requests for vegetarian dishes from *Diet for a Small Planet*. I was given as a gift *The Whole Earth Catalogue*. This compendium showed how to live on your own and grow your own foods. Oh, boy! Some were intent on saving the planet through food choices. But, after my Christmas dinner they seemed quite OK with Bill's favorite, an insanely rich seven-layer Hungarian dobos torte, made with a dozen eggs and a pound of butter. Trying to get on board with the new fads, I bought a yogurt maker for one to take back to school. I thought I was adapting. But I wasn't sure about their perception of Dad's new wife.

The biggest stepmother challenge was when his seventeen-year-old son came home from boarding school with a sixteen-year-old girlfriend. I later guided them to their separate bedrooms.

He said, "Oh no, we're sleeping together."

I was alarmed, but he was quite determined. Thinking it was so wrong to allow that, I called Bill into the fray. The two of us went into a closed-door discussion.

"This girl is only sixteen. I would never bring a guy to my parents' house to sleep over. That would have been insolent. The answer would have been a resounding no, but I would never have even dared."

"Well, he lives with his mother and she guides his mores and manners. I don't influence him there. Besides, I see him so seldom ... I don't want to cause a rift. I'll talk with them and see how this girl feels."

He came back, saying, "Well, they claim they've been together before at school, and she consents, so I said it was OK."

Exasperated, I railed at Bill. "This is not OK. It just isn't right. In fact, she is a minor." I felt invisible.

To make matters worse, the next day on the boat, she stripped off her bikini top. I gathered it was to show she wanted no boundaries on the boat, either.

One of the older guys in the stern said, "She needs a spanking." So, I wasn't the only one feeling the insolence.

Even though dramatic changes were taking place around sexuality in the early seventies, with "free love" and "If it feels good, do it," this issue suddenly was right in my face.

Parents like Bill were trying to be their kids' best friends, trying to understand them rather than direct their thinking. I got that, but it didn't sit well with me. "Parents should not be condoning sex with sixteen-year-olds in their own home." I groaned about how hurtful his open endorsement was to me since I disagreed so strongly. Didn't I count?

I thought he should have understood my protective feelings for women where sex was concerned, but I did not offer the lecture. For me, the generation gap seemed to be widening. At that moment, I realized how challenging it was to impact the lives of kids you didn't raise.

I was mad at both Bill and his son. For a moment, I tried being more open-minded than my parents would have been. But I just wasn't ready for blurred boundaries on this issue. The consequences for women of any age were always on my mind. They weren't in love—just experimenting. Not only was I exasperated not to have Bill's support on this, I felt left out of this decision … and I was his wife and it was now our home. Raising kids was challenging enough, but when there wasn't a united front, it could be complicated.

Another incident with my teenagers had me in an edgy spot. We had invited an executive from one of the top advertising agencies and his wife to dinner. Bill and Blair had raced together and had many sailing stories to share. I was looking forward to swapping advertising tales. The animated sailing yarns changed course abruptly when his teenage daughter came home and into the living room.

After introductions, she aggressively took over the conversation, grandstanding with talk about her favorite folk hero of the day, Abbie Hoffman. As she talked, it was as though she was giving them a short course on the counterculture, whether they wanted it or not. And to the head of an agency who made his living understanding and communicating to that market segment.

My cozy dinner had been to get to know them better. How was I to get the conversation away from Abbie Hoffman and back to advertising? Bill wasn't initiating any changes of subject, either. I could see the couple straining to be polite.

Never at a loss for words in a business setting, I was stunned at how inadequate I felt to deal with a teenager who was screaming to be seen and heard. I was stymied.

Later I asked Bill, "Why didn't you intervene to change the subject?

He said, "Sometimes you have to be the adult in the room. When kids act out, they have issues. Just let it go. You are the adult. Don't take it so personally."

Easy for him say. I had no experience with teens acting out. These kids were finding ways to assert themselves that would never have flown in my era. I was flummoxed and inexperienced about teens' needs and issues in these dramatically changing times. It seemed Bill wanted to err on the side of keeping them close rather than dealing with brash behavior, but I found my new role a bit bewildering. I wasn't the mother. I was the other. Then, to be fair, I remembered what I had brought home to my parents, a nightmare like few others would have to face. That thought was humbling. I needed to adapt again.

Often needing a sounding board besides Bill, I would go over to my friend Miriam's. She was a working stepmom with expansive professional working experiences. As career women and stepmoms, we had a lot in common. She lived nearby, so we saw each other often. I listened carefully as she reminded me, "You know that daughters living with their newly divorced dads often have issues." That gave me perspective.

Miriam was my friend and confidant. We celebrated many occasions together, best of all our birthdays. On one of my most memorable birthdays we were so engrossed in yakking and drinking wine one snowy December day that we didn't notice the gently falling snow had turned into a blizzard. When we finally left the restaurant in Chicago, we had to plod through snow drifts; the stairwell leading to the El was piled high so high with snow that we couldn't find the steps. When we finally got to our stop, we had to dig her car out of a snowbank. Driving to my street we found it impassable so I got out of the car in high heels and trudged through icy snow up to my knees, shoes squishing with each painful step. But we never missed our birthday dinners.

The first time Miriam and her husband came for dinner, she brought me Milan Kundera's *The Unbearable Lightness of Being*. That was the beginning of many discussions about books. She and I would sneak off to the many book alleys in and around our college town. She knew the best and even the rare bookstores since our town is where she worked on her Ph.D. I learned from her how to read a single author intensively and to seek hard-to-find editions. But, with all those dinners and walks and talks, I never shared my own personal journey.

When Bill's kids came home each summer, my crash course in campus culture would begin. Home to peacefully sail on Lake Michigan, they often floated their own stories of protests, canceled classes, and dislocation as they moved about from campus to campus. Their lives were filled with tales of hitchhiking and one even living in a commune for a stint. It all sounded far different from my subdued college days sitting around listening to the quiet strumming of a guitar to lyrics of the Kingston Trio. I felt the depth of the generational gap especially when their drug-laced music radiated from the boat each summer.

In spite of all their disruptions on campus and different lifestyles, there was a sprightly energy that flowed from each of these kids. Campus life as I knew it had changed dramatically. I wondered how they dealt with unwanted sex or if it was even an issue. There were freedoms on campus I had never experienced. No curfews for them. They were unleashed. They were experimenting with life. They were independent in ways we had never been. What a change.

Each of his kids shared their own risky adventures, but I would not dare bring up my own campus calamity. In these days of new sexual liberties, would they relate to the huge consequences of unwanted pregnancy in my day? Theirs was a world of unfettered freedoms, free love, lots of weed, and rock concerts. They had the birth control pill. My times had been filled with restraint, taboos, and restrictions. Could they begin to understand the circumstances I and so many women my age lived through? Probably not. I was feeling my way into this new world of freedoms with a dynamic young family in ever-changing times.

Chapter Twenty-One

Tasting Activism

B efore Bill and I were married, I was just a quiet observer of the political and social scenes swirling around me. The year 1968 was one of the most tumultuous years America had ever seen. Mainly because of the polarization of the war in Vietnam. Suddenly my life was filled with a kind of political activism I had never experienced.

Although his own business absorbed him, Bill always took time for political activism. We took trips to Washington, D.C., to lobby Congressmen against the war. He also organized the communications industry into a group opposing the Vietnam War.

At our home we hosted events and fascinating personalities of the day. Many were outspoken opponents of the war. One was Studs Terkel, the oral historian known for recording ordinary Americans telling their own stories. Studs was the real thing in Chicago in those days. Perceived as a man of the people, he had the unique skill of tenderly extracting personal commentaries for his radio audience.

One evening my eyes and ears were opened to the incredible power of storytelling when Studs came into our living room to tape his radio show. I had heard his soothing voice come over the radio, but in person he projected the image of kindly white-haired grandfather. He softly approached the group of young, clean-cut military men from West Point and Annapolis, called the Concerned Academy Graduates, and began slowly by having them identify their backgrounds and experiences. All had combat experiences in Vietnam, one was a doctor and lieutenant commander in the Navy, one was an infantry commander in the Marines, and one was a captain in the secretive Phoenix Program. All attended the most prestigious military academies in the country. Studs skillfully pulled from each of them their own horrendous experiences as combat veterans.

"What was it like for you as a medic when villages were lit up with incendiary bombs?"

His questions and demeanor allowed him to get these young men to recount in exquisite detail their horrific experiences while revealing the strong emotions that led to their eventual resignation of their military careers.

You could observe their pain being lanced as each delivered passionate stories recreating scenes from behind the lines. As their emotions flowed freely, their amazing strength of character would shine through. They were emotionally conflicted as sons of former distinguished military families. Their fathers and grandfathers were decorated men of past battles.

Seated on our sofas that evening, listening to the suffering and injustices they had experienced, all of our eyes filled with tears. Here were some of the country's finest warriors, speaking out passionately and honestly about the atrocities of this war, and risking their careers and futures to do so. I was spellbound.

Years later Studs told me, "I never forgot the bravery of those guys coming forward as they did at that time." His oral histories and commentaries became legendary over the years. Who would not like to have a chat with this white-haired man with the mellifluous tones in his voice. For his deeply moving interviews, he eventually won a Pulitzer for his work with the book *The Good War* in 1985—all through the power of storytelling.

Another guest of ours was Bill Kunstler, the infamous lead defense attorney in the Chicago Seven Conspiracy Trial. Just as charming in person as in court, this colorful icon presided over what became the trial of the century. With his gravelly voice and huge Einstein-like hair, he was quite a spectacle in court as he defended the guys accused of causing the riots at the 1968 Democratic Convention. He looked somewhat like the hippies he was trying to defend.

Behind-the-scene details of the day were repeated with dramatic exuberance when Bill Kunstler stayed with us as a guest during the trial. He was just as entertaining in person as he was in court, and he exercised a quick wit. I loved his overtly ribald sense of humor that was even more candid when not in court.

When Kunstler walked into court, Judge Julius Hoffman's stage, he had colorful characters like Jerry Rubin and Abbie Hoffman of the hip antiwar cult to defend as well as intellectual activists promoting non-violent social change like Dave Dellinger and Tom Hayden. They were strong personalities known to the anti-war movement. In the courtroom they caused mayhem. Once they appeared in judicial robes. When Judge Hoffman ordered them to remove the robes they did so, only to reveal Chicago police uniforms underneath. The media loved the courtroom antics. It was a spectacle, and we loved having Kunstler as our guest to add even more behind-the-scenes color.

One of many amusing points in the trial was when Bill Kunstler reported to Judge Hoffman, "Your honor, what appears to be marijuana has been sent in the mail to Abbie Hoffman."

The judge said, "I am sure you can take care of that matter without troubling the court."

"Your honor," Kunstler responded, "I will personally see that it is burned this evening." There was much hooting in the courtroom. Later a movie was produced depicting all the courtroom antics using the exact script of the proceedings.

All this political activism was electrifying. I was expanding my views, especially about people struggling to be heard.

My own heartbeat issues of the times centered around women's rights. And how could I not feel the pain of women without rights to make their own decisions. Suffering as I had from sexual assault, stripped of pride, my self-esteem in tatters and shame that should not have been mine to own, I felt their pain. My experience left me feeling strongly supportive of women seeking to choose their own destiny without societal pressures. Times were changing.

Finally, in 1973, with all the marches and protests by courageous women, the Roe v. Wade case legalized abortion. At last women had a say over what happened to them and their bodies. Pregnancy was in their hands. They would not need to shrink under the stigma of shame or illegitimacy. They could stand tall. Political activism apparently paid off. In light of what I had to endure, this was a monumental decision for all women. Social activism had opened my eyes. I had grown with the times.

Chapter Twenty-Two

A Reversal of Roles

M y dear sister Judy was never able to break the yoke of a struggling single mother. I saw her plowing through life with such difficulty, such weight on her shoulders. Earlier Judy's role had been my mentor, my brilliant sister, my tutor. Now she was my shadow, following after me. When I moved to Chicago, she begged to come, too, even though she didn't yet have a job or a place to stay. I felt the need to take her under my wing.

She had been there for me in my darkest moments. I owed her. "OK. Come to Chicago, and we will get a place together," I'd told her. My job was absorbing in those early months, and with all my travel, I thought it just might work. It was nice to have family close in a city when I knew so few people.

Just a few short years before, Judy had been an aspiring student at an exclusive college for women, but she had somehow managed to slip off her upward trajectory. It was a puzzle I never solved. In high school she was an overachiever, but in college she was not on a good path. I knew this because we still shared a bedroom at home, and I would overhear details of her dating escapades. Even though I was three years younger, I sensed her judgment in men was questionable. Her top priority, instead of her studies, was this guy from Kenyon College.

From the very beginning he impressed me as an insensitive effete. His pretentiousness even made Judy feel uncomfortable. He grew up in Shaker Heights, Ohio, an exclusive suburb where the city planners made sure all houses were monitored to fit the right codes in color and appearance. Appearance was everything to the mother who raised him. Judy told me tales about her insistence he wear a suit jacket at dinner. Apparently being proper was paramount to him and his mother. However, in our family home, his brand of supposedly gracious behavior was off putting. He exuded a sense of superiority that cost him my respect, but apparently not hers.

The incident that made me wince was when he let his suitcase roll down our stairway, laughing all the while as it smashed into the wall at the bottom, leaving a gash. Even I could see how immature he was. What a jerk. That same weekend he wanted me to double-date with a friend of his, also from Kenyon. Judy encouraged me to go along. This aggressive, wisecracking friend of his kept trying to paw my breasts while we drove to a movie. At sixteen, I wasn't fair game for this brash college guy, and I was furious with Judy and her new boyfriend. What did she see in either of them?

I was stunned when a few months later she ran off to marry this slacker. It left the family flabbergasted. Soon we learned about her pregnancy.

Now, with Judy divorced and with a toddler to care for, we three lived together in a small studio apartment in the heart of the Near North. All went well … for a while.

One day when I was trying to cash my paycheck at our local grocery, the manager told me he wouldn't cash it. "Your sister's checks bounce, and I don't want to take the risk." I was furious. It was the most convenient way to cash a check from work, and now my own credit was in question. This was long before credit cards and when cash was king.

"Why didn't you tell me you were cashing bad checks?" I demanded. She just shrugged it off. Her behavior was puzzling and frightening. We were raised to be honest. What had happened to her? It was deeply unsetting.

Living with a toddler added a lot of sparkle to our lives. Her daughter Lorna would say, "Aunt Merry bring me home ice cream or you will get tickled all night." She not only added a touch of reality to my unreal, zany days at the publishing house but was a joy in my life. At night she would crawl into my lap, showing me her puppets or her drawings, or she would show off her improvised dances. She was just a few years older than Ann would be. I hoped Ann was having an easier life than Lorna, not cramped in a studio apartment.

It was Judy's judgment in men that bothered me yet again. Although she had snagged an office job at one of the leading consulting firms, filled with single men, she could only hook up with the married ones. When I asked her about it, she said, "Who wants to date a woman with a child? The guys in my office are looking for swinging singles."

In those early years while Judy was working, Lorna experienced trauma after trauma. Her finger got pinched in an elevator door at the YWCA where she waited for Judy, and she was rushed to the hospital for stitches. Then, she came down with a bad case of pneumonia. After leaving Lorna in the hospital overnight, Judy didn't come home. I waited up, fretting about what to do. When she didn't show by morning, either, I raced to the hospital myself to find Lorna alone in her room in an oxygen tent trying to eat breakfast by herself. I was furious. When Judy finally arrived, I railed, "Where have you been? How could you not be here when she needed you?" Apparently, she had been with some married guy from her office.

I knew it was rough for Judy to meet men, but her priorities had me exasperated. I realized, painfully and slowly, that she was conflicted with both love and regret over having Lorna. She did love Lorna dearly but resented she could not have the kind of dating life I was having. It saddened me to see that life had ground down her self-respect and drive. She should have finished college, especially with her good academics.

Still, I kept Judy and Lorna close, in that studio apartment, for three years. Secretly, I felt vindicated that I had not tried to raise a child on my own and grateful that I had accepted her early advice. Yet, I still wanted to help her and Lorna. We were family. But, it was getting complicated.

Lorna was spunky, and there were many really fun moments living with a small person. Some were awkward, such as when I had my dates come to that small studio apartment to pick me up. Lorna said to one, "My aunt stayed out really late last night. Are you going to stay out late, too?"

Disasters seemed to always shadow Judy. One Christmas Eve, with her company check in her purse, she was mugged and robbed of her Christmas bonus on her way home. After her those heady high school years when she was a class leader, life was no longer a lift.

Over the years and well beyond our life in that cramped little studio apartment, I kept them close, hosting all Lorna's birthdays, holidays, recitals, graduations, and key celebrations.

When my own son was born, Judy was more content with herself and immediately attached herself to him like a mother bear protecting her cub. She indulged him and adopted him as her own, coming to babysit him as often as possible. Billy loved that Aunt Judy would never quite say where they were going, but the two would sneak off to see *Beverly Hills Cops* over and over again. He was fascinated with the swear words and swagger in the film, and she indulged him. She never hid the fact that he was her favorite. She would come often to my house to steal him away for movies, ice cream, and whatever adventures they cooked up together. It had been wonderful to have Judy and Lorna close.

What I will never, ever forget is that Judy was always there for me and especially when I most needed her. She shielded me from shame and gave me permission not to end up raising a child when I wasn't ready. She had not been ready herself and wanted to spare me the same. We were as close as two sisters could ever be, in spite of our spats. Years later when she moved to Florida and I to California, we talked on the phone every week of our lives. In spite of our differences, she was always my touchstone.

Chapter Twenty-Three

Dreamscapes 1972

———— ∿ ————

Being attached to Lorna as I had been, I knew the joy children could add to your life. I was in no rush, however, to have my own since Bill's and my new life together was exciting and full of rich experiences.

Over time I could not help but notice Bill's easy rapport with kids wherever we were. His affinity for children actually began, he told me, when consoling the other kids in his orphan home. That interest led to studying psychology at the University of Chicago, where he became a counselor in Bruno Bettelheim's residential treatment center for disturbed kids. "Working with these kids, I saw they weren't disturbed; they just needed attention—just like the orphans," he said. He loved little people, as he called them, and I knew instinctively it was time for me to become a mom, not just a stepmom.

Although we'd never discussed having a family, I knew it was OK. But, when he commented, "I am so happy it's just the two of us," I had to think twice. I knew our relationship had been a reprieve from his messy divorce and the responsibilities of raising four other children. But after two years of "just us," I became joyously pregnant.

Pregnancy with jubilation is far different from pregnancy with shame. Now, I could allow myself to embrace pregnancy and the full thrill of motherhood. I was overjoyed.

A week past my due date, I was insufferably big and uncomfortable in the stifling June heat. Wearing an oversized shirt, I shuffled around in my slippers to make the morning coffee. My mother had been here a week already, driving me crazy. "Let me make the coffee," she said, making me feel useless once again.

As the summer sun poured into the kitchen, Bill knelt on the floor, busily arranging bags of sails for his sailboat. It was Saturday; yacht racing took place whether babies were born or not. His library was filled with sailing books— Chichester's *Gypsy Moth*, Joseph Conrad's *Tales of the Sea*, *Taiki, Two Against Cape Horn*, and loads of other adventures. He came over and hugged me. "Is it OK if I go today? Are you feeling any different?"

"Go, enjoy your race," I said. "We'll leave messages if we have an emergency run to the hospital."

After he left, I decided to clean the garage. Trying to feel useful, I was waddling around a wet garage, hose in hand, when my mother poked her head out and said, "Are you crazy?" Maybe that physical activity triggered the contractions, but anyhow, they were real. I called my doctor, who said, "You should probably come into the hospital now."

Once there, the contractions were not getting closer together, and I started to worry. The clock on the wall seemed to tick by ever so slowly. I remembered how long labor can be. Judy rushed in with a basket of her own comfort remedies. One was a root beer float, my favorite growing up, but the ice cream had melted long ago. Her sense of timing was always a bit off, but her nurturing heart was golden. When we were teens, she always took so long getting ready for church, I would just leave without her. As she slid into the pew after the service had started, she would quietly pinch me hard for leaving without her. Today, though, instead of trying to squash me as the tag-along little sis, she was acting like a pilot fish, by my side at every turn. She desperately wanted to be with me for this birth, remembering how no one was there at my side ten years earlier. There was joy in the air this time.

Judy and Mom knew how much I had suffered that first time around, through the abandonment and the cruel adoptive process. They weren't there when I had to face the long labor and the bigger pain of handing over my baby. Those events from the past were never spoken about, but I was grateful they were here now. They soothed me with drinks, crackers, and their own funny stories. Judy was busy leaving messages for Bill and worrying how to get to him. After a point, my doctor decided that inducing labor was the way to go. Would Bill get here in time? It was late in the afternoon by now; surely the race was over.

Hours went by. Dazed from the long labor, I looked over and saw Bill in green scrubs, looking in from the doorway. This was rare for the time; doctors forty years ago didn't like fathers fainting in the delivery room. But Bill was standing by to give encouragement. I was thrilled that he would see the birth after all.

By that time the epidural had kicked in, and I was no longer in that deep, dull pain. I was more than ready for this long process to be over. With encouraging words from the team and one final push, my baby was born, and euphoria set in.

As women know, the pain of delivery is forgotten once you see that tiny human being blinking in the bright lights.

"It's a boy," the doctor beamed, holding him up for me to see. I kept stretching my neck to see where they had put him and saw a rosy pink baby with bright open eyes as he was being bathed. "Are his eyes blue?" I asked. They were intense and the shape resembled mine, even as a tiny newborn. Seeing his tightly curled fists and little feet kicking was beyond thrilling. I was so thankful that Bill was there to share the moment. This time, I wasn't alone and there was joy instead of sadness. It was magical.

When I finally held him, I felt like a mother lion with her cub, wanting to lick his perfect little ears. Wow. Those mothering instincts are powerful.

I was basking in the joy of the whole experience but was exhausted from the long labor and ready for much needed sleep.

After hugs and kisses and great excitement, the family quietly stole out of my hospital room. Drained but exhilarated, I fell into a rich deep sleep, but woke up suddenly in a sweat.

It wasn't just a bad dream but a nightmare, and I never had nightmares. I felt that someone in a dark overcoat had come into the hospital room and taken my baby.

In a panic, I called the nurse, saying, "Please go and check if my baby is OK. I had a bad dream that he wasn't."

I tossed from side to side in the bed and was still sweating when she returned and said, "Yes, he's sleeping soundly. He is OK."

Relief coursed through me. My body finally relaxed, and I fell peacefully back to sleep.

In the morning, I recalled it all in great detail and thought it must have been my protective hormones kicking in, like a mother bird fluttering and scolding when you approach her nest. It seemed natural to feel so protective. At that moment, it was my logical conclusion.

It was not the right conclusion at all. Only now, as I look back and better understand my deeply hidden feelings, does that dream make sense. Allowing my subconscious to dig back into my raw and confused emotions surrounding the birth of Ann, I realize I was remembering, deep inside, the time my baby was taken from me in another hospital, on a very gray day. I will never be able to wipe away that act of severance.

Chapter Twenty-Four

The Telling

———~~———

Rather than share the story that shook my very foundation, I just went on living my life. I never had the courage to bear my soul to others. Neither the campus assault nor the birth and adoption were ever mentioned in my family again. They were erased—not forgotten, just buried. My family was no different from others facing the same dilemma in my day. It was a social stigma on us all.

Just before Bill and I were married, feeling more emotionally secure, I pondered peeling back those dark layers with him. Not sure how to approach this difficult topic one evening I casually asked, "Why are you enmeshed in so much political activity?"

"Probably because of my early days in an orphan home.

We were so poor during the Depression that I would run along the railroad tracks picking up coal that fell off the cars to take home to heat our house. Mother couldn't raise three boys after Dad died, so off we went. After the orphan home I went right into the Army during World War II. There I saw how mistreated Blacks were, the ones serving alongside me. Injustice deeply disturbs me now.

That was my opening. He had revealed his caring nature. Feeling his compassion, I decided to tell Bill my story. I felt he would not judge me the way the outside world of the early sixties had. With him I was no longer distancing myself. So, that night, wrapped up in his arms on the sofa, it just felt like the right time.

"There was an incident my senior year in college," I began. He sat there listening but saying little, rubbing my arms as I started through all the layers of my story.

At each new turn in my story, I twisted the handkerchief he had handed me at the first sight of tears. I plodded on through my whole journey, the painful discussions with my parents, the isolation, and the birth that was marred by torment and shame.

He squeezed me gently, saying, "You were so brave to bear that alone."

When I came to the saddest moment, handing my baby over for adoption, I choked up. "That is my deepest pain of all." My sniffling turned to a flood of tears, something Bill can't bear to see, even now so many years later.

By then he could see how raw and emotional I still was. As I struggled to finish the story, he kept wiping my tears away. I could see he felt my anguish, probably because he, too, had suffered isolation and pain. He understood.

It was exhausting to walk him through my feelings that were still deeply buried. But I felt so relieved to share my whole story. As he held me closely that night, my pain receded, and I felt very connected to him. I wasn't alone with my secret anymore.

Over the years, I masked that birth with blinders, trying to shut off any maternal memory or emotion. My only reminder was when doctors would ask, "How many children do you have? How many live births?" I always hesitated. This shame of giving a child away was stuffed down and not shared easily.

As Billy was growing up, I would periodically think of Ann and how to reach her. Occasionally I would stop and count the years, thinking about how old she would be. When Billy was about seven, I decided to track down Marion. Knowing Ann was in her delicate teenage years, I was not sure if calling was a good idea. At least Marion could tell me how she was doing. Closing the door to my bedroom, I nervously dialed the number. Instead of Marion answering, it was someone else. Not knowing what to say next, I just hung up and never tried again. I always thought it would be unfair to her new parents to try and enter her life, but I was curious.

Very unexpectedly, I did share my story with my friend Miriam. It wasn't at all planned. I dropped by her home to chat as I often did. Her home was like going into a library with shelves filled to the ceiling with books, many covering subjects she was teaching at the time. Her love of learning was so strong that she left the business world to became a professor. Beloved by her students they nominated her for teacher of the year in Illinois, an honor that was eventually bestowed. I knew Miriam best as the kind of friend you could call at 4 a.m. with a problem. And I did just that when our sons were teenagers. With her tremendous capacity for understanding people, she would be the first one I would ask for advice. I never shared my deepest secret with her until this one day.

We were, as usual, sitting around her kitchen table—the very table noted in a story she had written and published called "The Kitchen."[1] Handed me a story she had written

---

[1] Ben-Yoseph, M and Rosen, D. (Eds.) (2009). Where We Find Ourselves: Jewish Women Around the World Write About Home, Albany, NY: Suny Press pp.21-24

which began, "If you come to my house in Evanston, sooner or later you will spend time in my kitchen. This is my favorite spot in the house, maybe because 'home' means first of all 'kitchen' to me."

As I read her story, sitting in her kitchen, I felt she was serving me a cup of real truth instead of her lemon tea. The story went on about her own childhood kitchen in Romania: "The kitchen was the heart and soul of not only my family, but all the other families who shared it with us after the communists had nationalized our house and we had to share it with others."

I knew that her father, a prominent banker, became a political prisoner and their family home had been occupied. She recounts in the story, "A highly placed party member and his wife moved upstairs into our guest room. When he was not drunk, he liked to recite poems dedicated to the communist party. He cited these poems with great fervor and in a very loud voice and nobody ever dared to complain." Miriam was just fifteen, and the next part was especially painful.

"One night, after leaving the kitchen not because it was late but because I had a field trip with my class early the next day, I woke up because I felt someone touching me. He was sitting on my bed and I had no idea how long he had been there. I was terrified. I must have tried to shout or say something because he got up from my bed almost immediately and told me that my mother would go to prison just like my father if I dared say anything. And I had not for thirty-five years."

It hit me like a bolt. Despite knowing Miriam well for so many years, she had never told me that story. I did know her pain in losing her father, but not this secret pain. While in prison, her dad suffered several heart attacks and was kept there without the opportunity of a trial. After suffering a fatal heart attack, Miriam and her mother fled to begin a new life in a country where neither spoke the language.

Hearing her horrendous story, I took a deep breath. With uncontrollable emotion, I was shedding tears for her and what she had suffered, as well as tears for me. I now needed to share my story.

"Miriam, you don't know what I suffered just as I was graduating college."

Apparently, there was anguish etched over my face. I was shaking with pent-up emotions. They all came pouring out at once.

As she consoled me and calmed me down a bit, she gently said, "You need to get these feelings out, write them down, as I have. That is too much to have bottled up, and obviously you are still hurting."

She continued. "Storytelling," she said, "is more than a way of communicating; it is cathartic."

Miriam successfully published her stories from Romania, and I admired her courage. But that conversation in her kitchen was many years ago, and still I wrote nothing. In spite of all the blank journals Miriam gave me and all her encouragement, I never wrote one word of my story down.

I just went on living with that hole in my heart, not really knowing how to acknowledge the fact that I had given away a child. It was a pain I would return to at the strangest times. Just driving on a country road with Bill, out of nowhere I would start crying, recounting, once again, my deepest regret. There was still a knot deep in my gut. Bill would soothe me with comforting words, but the pain never went away.

Thinking that giving up a child was somehow a crack in my character, a tarnish, it was the one chapter in my life best to be deleted—just reinforced by silence. My family never revisited that chapter. My feelings about it were never questioned or validated.

How I wish now that I'd had a conversation with my mother long ago, beginning with, "If you were so miserable waiting ten years for your firstborn, and losing two stillborn babies, why didn't you share your thoughts about how I would feel giving one away?"

That afternoon my trembling body revealed just then how much pain was still locked inside.

Chapter Twenty-Five

The Hardest Conversation 1993

‹‹‹‹‹‹

Years later when Billy was a college student, I was thinking it might be time to have that hard conversation. As mother and son we were very close, but he didn't yet know the secret I had been avoiding.

When he was younger, I could not bring myself to share a rape story. I couldn't taint the image of his mother by revealing such painful details. But when I heard about fraternity hazing rituals or speed-drinking at Berkeley, I was concerned. I needed to tell him about my own college nightmare, but how and when?

We were a closely knit team. When he was probably around age seven he'd said, "You know mom, we can't trust Dad. He was divorced before." That spoke volumes about how important stability is to kids. I would not bring up my own past. Not yet.

When he was about thirteen, he and I took an impromptu trip to Italy. I chose Italy mainly because it had been the focus of his study in school that year. It was a crazy trip through the Italian countryside, mainly because of two colorful women who always kept the bus waiting with outrageous, hilarious excuses. Billy thought Mary Lu and Hazel were pure entertainment. They regaled him with their stories: "The hotel rooms are so small I have to slide off the bed and twist my fanny around to sit on the toilet."

He was a great traveler and very observant about Italian men. "Mom, that taxi driver never zeroed the meter." "Mom, did you see what the bus driver does when the women climb the steps into the bus? He scoops his hand behind their butts. See? Watch him." The tour was pretty boring for a kid, so one day I suggested we ditch it and head back to the hotel, which had a pool.

As we entered the lobby of this small, charming hotel outside of Florence, with its usual green shutters, its stucco, and its roses climbing the trellis, I asked the overly friendly concierge at the front desk, "You have a pool here, don't you?" The lobby was empty; everyone seemed to be off touring. He said, "It's on the roof terrace. Is madame planning to go up now?" Why should he care when we went to the pool?

Just the way he drawled "madame" set off a small alarm. I told Billy as we walked to our room, "Don't be surprised if we have company at the pool. After we changed, I said "Let's wait for a few minutes."

At the pool, Billy jumped in, practicing his laps as he did on swim team, when the concierge appeared. He came over to me and pulled up a chair. He reached over and tried taking my hand, saying, "I thought madame looked a bit lonely." He was creepy, and I was trying to politely shoo him away. As we were talking, I sensed a shadow over my shoulder. It was Billy, dripping wet but stepping silently into our space like a sentry, just standing there without saying a word. He didn't need to. The concierge soon walked away.

While he was in high school, I did my best to shield him from boozy teenage escapades. I would bounce out of bed when I heard the front door opening at night and come into the kitchen and say, "So?" I loved to hear about his adventures of the night. I'd fix a snack, and we'd sit at the kitchen table for a while, chatting about his night. I might give him a hug to see if I detected alcohol and see how his story lined up. Knowing one friend of his flipped his car over while driving drunk, I was just checking. Also, I knew that he and his high school friends would sneak out Thursday nights, piling into a car and heading (I overheard him say on the phone) to Thirsty Thursdays. Once I followed them in my car to see where Thirsty Thursdays, was but their trail went cold. It wasn't until years later that I learned our local Holiday Inn was serving these underage kids, who looked old enough to be college students. He and his friends were apparently tapping into happy hour and passing themselves off as college students. They fooled me as well.

Back then, Billy watched out for me, too. Once my friend Caroline, a caterer who knew about a much-acclaimed restaurant opening that night, invited me there for a drink. It wasn't far from my office, so I walked until I saw the sign she'd described, a giant tomato beckoning all to enter this new food emporium. Scoozi was a hot new Italian restaurant then. (I later learned that Stephen Colbert worked as a waiter there one summer after attending Northwestern University.) It was the place to be that night.

Inside, the grand opening was well underway. I waited patiently, but Caroline was late. So I went to the new, elongated bar—a trend in those days, designed for eating as well as drinking. They were serving up small Margherita pizzas—the thin-crust pizza was new and a big contrast to the popular deep-dish, Chicago-style pizza. Still no Caroline, so I sat at the bar and ordered a glass of wine. This big, expansive bar, friendly and inviting, reminded me of those I had seen in

Europe. A while later I phoned Billy to tell him I would be a bit late. Bill was out of town, and he was home alone.

When I dialed our number from a phone booth by the bar, Billy apparently heard the clanking of glasses and the spirited tone and said, "Mom, where are you?" I explained that it was a restaurant opening. With the bar scene getting noisier by the minute, he said, "Mom, I think you need to come home now." When I hung up I smiled to myself at his protective nature. We looked out for each other!

Now, he was a tall, handsome college kid with cobalt blue eyes, partying in his fraternity at the other end of the country, away from my prying eyes.

Home for Christmas freshman year, he and his friends were jumping out of their skin to have a holiday party at our house. I was all for it, but I wasn't sure how to control the alcohol they wanted to serve. I knew that booze flowed freely at college, but I wasn't about to have my home become an open bar.

I told his friends, when they were sitting in my kitchen, "I'll host only if I can make a light Champagne punch and control the liquor, or, no party." They agreed.

The night of the party, I observed a huge transformation in all of them. Dressed in shirts and ties, the guys were showing manners I had not seen in high school. The girls, dressed in heels and skirts, hugged them warmly and traded campus stories through the night. I was thinking they had finally grown up and out of their high school pranks. Then I saw one friend attempting to pour pints of Bourbon and vodka into my punch bowl. Although the party went off without incident, I saw their thirst had increased at college, from beer to hard alcohol. I was not apprehensive about drug use with this group—many were good athletes—but I was nervous now about their alcohol consumption.

This is the point where I should have had that talk with Billy about alcohol and dating, but I didn't. It wasn't until he invited his dad and me to homecoming at his fraternity that I decided we definitely needed to have the talk I had put off for years. Walking along campus that weekend hearing the thumping drumbeat of the band and girls calling out to Billy, I felt happy he had settled well into campus life. It reminded me of my happy college times, until that one night.

At his frat house, a friend from high school and now a fraternity brother as well, came bounding down the stairs with a beer bottle in hand. "Hi, Mrs. B," he said, giving me a hug.

With a youthful shock of hair over one eye, he was still boyishly good looking. I watched him then lean against a wall with one leg pulled up behind him, thumb in his jean pocket. He struck this stance with a certain posed panache and gestured to a pretty coed with his beer bottle like it was a baton. It was hard for me to reconcile this new confidence with the boy who used to shyly tiptoe into my kitchen and lift the lids on my stove to see what I was cooking. Where did this new bravado with women come from? As he eventually draped one arm over her shoulder, I wondered if it was the beer giving him this new swagger. Just physically being in Billy's fraternity, I thought of Pete and the license he took with me. Fraternity life, I knew, was filled with boozy parties. I needed to have that long-overdue talk about drinking and fraternity life. Women and alcohol gave me bad vibes in this setting. I began plotting.

On a quiet Sunday afternoon, with rain splattering the windows in my apartment, this seemed to be the right time and place. My story would be a shock to him, and very uncomfortable to tell. I was dreading it.

Before he came I created a warm atmosphere by lighting the fireplace. It cast a warm glow over the room and the raindrops added a soothing rhythm of pings on the window. When he came in, we sat on the floor in front of the fire. I was facing him so I could watch his reaction. Twisting my scarf as I talked, I timidly began the story that began on my college campus when I was just about to graduate. "Waking up that morning and trying to piece together the night before was chilling. I didn't know at first where I had been. Where was that dark stairwell? Where were my friends? I had only flashbacks. Nothing was making sense."

Looking into his eyes the whole time, I continued, "That night, celebrating the end of finals at a campus tavern, turned my life into a nightmare."

As I tiptoed through my story, skipping some of the more painful details, he sat in stunned silence. I could read that this was more information than he would like to have about his mother. His body shifted uncomfortably with the weight of my story. Then he became very still.

When telling the part of having to tell my dad, his grandpa, his eyes turned misty. His grandpa was very special to Billy, not the raging bull he appeared when I was growing up. My dad had softened over the years, and he adored Billy. They had a special bond.

And yet, Billy could challenge his grandpa. When he was just seven, with the family huddled in the den watching the nightly news on television, watching a race riot my Dad had said, "Just look at those n_____."

There was an awkward silence, broken by Billy saying, "Grandpa, we don't say that word in this house." I was so proud of him.

I would never have dared take on my Dad so directly, but this comment was skillfully delivered like a knife through butter.

When Gramps came to visit us, in what would become his last year of life, he and Billy would stay up late debating timely topics. Billy was just twelve when he and his gramps wrangled late into the night about "the draft" and "the morality of taking a life through euthanasia."

On the subject of "life," Billy argued, "It's all you really have, grandpa. Your life. Why would you want to give up?" Billy was strongly against the draft, while Dad argued it was a man's duty to defend his country.

The next morning Dad said, "That Billy is really bright. He can really hold his own." Dad cherished their time together that summer and sent him a baseball mitt that Billy treasured. When Dad died, Billy wrote the most loving story about his grandpa and that glove ending with "and I never saw my grandpa again."

Sitting spellbound, Billy listened to me painfully describe my complicated predicament—to a parent, his granddad, when I was about his age—of an unwanted pregnancy.

"It was an agonizing." Dad left, went upstairs, and started to cry. Through tears, he said to me, 'You are not a toy.' I could tell he felt the sting and depth of the injustice."

"What did Grandma say?" Mom had come to stay with Billy whenever we traveled. It was the greatest gift she could have given me, the comfort to go abroad knowing everything would be OK.

"Your grandma was a tough lady. She adjusted fast and did not want me to be sent to one of those homes for unwed mothers where you quietly disappeared behind tall secretive walls. Instead, she made sure I could have a fresh new start, in a private home. She stood by me."

Sparing the details of giving birth, I simply ended with the finale of having a baby girl, all alone in a distant hospital. It was rough for him to process, I could tell. He squirmed a lot. Revisiting my grief of handing over a child, his sister, was especially painful. Telling him was excruciating

By the time I was finished, my emotions were rubbed raw. Choking with emotion, I could hardly get the words out but ended with, "So, somewhere out there you have a sister."

"How old would she be now?" he asked.

"Ten years older than you. Over the years, I would always stop and wonder to myself, how old is Ann now?" She was lost, but not forgotten, I told him.

Sitting dumbfounded by the weight of my story, Billy tried to lighten things up.

"I always wanted an older sister." But I could see the gravity of my story taking hold of him.

He'd been staring at the floor, his body slouched over. Finally looking up, he said, "Oh, Mom, what a nightmare for you."

We both had tears in our eyes, but I was so relieved to have finally told the truth. There was so much more to share with Billy that afternoon, but after dropping such a chilling story on him about his mom, I just wasn't up for it. I wanted to regain some shred of dignity at that moment. Letting the story settle in on him was enough for one day.

Thinking back to that afternoon, I should have gone on to discuss the ramifications of sex and alcohol and the importance of consent. Talking openly about respect and dignity is the discussion mothers should have with sons. Relationships, with or without alcohol, should never be coercive and the emotional wellbeing of both engaging partners is important.

The double-standard in my day allowed men no consequences for unwanted sex. Women paid the emotional price.

My generation was not used to having conversations with their sons or daughters about sexual behavior. Just as my parents before, sex was not often mentioned. Sex education was gleaned from friends and older sisters. Without a big sister to ask, I think Billy probably learned his coming-of-age strategies from his friends, and movies like *The Breakfast Club* and *Fast Times at Ridgemont High*. Those were more authentic depictions of what adolescents talked about. We weren't talking to him much about sex, but the filmmakers sure were.

Emotionally exhausted, I felt relieved. That painful part of his mother's life was finally revealed, and the telling actually brought me peace.

Chapter Twenty-Six

Interrupted Tranquility

———

I had finally left behind the anguish and uncertainty of my earlier life. The faster paced city life was replaced with a retreat to the suburbs. Embracing motherhood with as much gusto as I had my career, I nestled Billy on my bicycle handlebars and rode to meet Bill's train. He would flash a big smile, saying, "Oh, my little love bugs," and would hoist Billy onto his back to walk home. Being a Mom added to my tranquility.

Feeling very much at ease as a suburban mom, my life seemed full enough until an advertising agency called to entice me back to work. Would I dare? How would this change our family dynamics? Would our close-knit life just split apart?

I wrestled with why I should even entertain the idea of becoming a working mom. I hadn't even been looking. But Bill's business had been hit hard by the cataclysmic Arabic oil embargo; times were tough, but he kept paying his employees, even though there was very little business coming into his firm. At that moment I decided to help and said "yes" to the job with the ad agency. Little did I know about the pressures parenting would present me as a working mom. I was about to be tested.

Daycare was a dilemma. Few daycare centers existed then. The center I found that fit our needs best said, "Can't pick up your child one minute after six." Luckily, the ad agency was in the same building as Bill's office, so we could come and go together. When it was almost five o'clock, I would duck out of client meetings with absurd excuses. It was embarrassing because most important client meetings took place late in the day. My boss would graciously cover for me, but for how long?

Streamlining my workday, I was always scheming for an early getaway. I was multitasking, a term not yet common, by making grocery lists under the table in meetings. With all the hyper-activities of building ad campaigns in the background and spontaneous last-minute meetings, those early departures were getting harder to pull off.

The pressure to get there through Chicago's ice and sleet, flat tires, and late client phone calls all made for a wild dash to the daycare center. Once I was there, the teachers were agitated if I couldn't get there in time for a debriefing of Billy's activities. I felt caught between two worlds.

Our tranquil home life was seriously tested. The part of being a working mom that rocked me most over the years was those unpredictable emergency calls from the daycare center and, later, his schools.

"Someone hit Billy in the nose with a baseball bat on the playground."

"This is the police department; your son was hit by a car on his bicycle. He's OK, but please go to the ER. He is fine, but a bit scratched up."

Or the time I called him when he got home from a summer day camp and he said, "Stop calling me; the ringing phone hurts my head." Arriving home, I found not only the suspected fever but a red line going up his leg. The doctor said, "Meet me in the emergency room right away. That's blood poisoning from his plantar wart." Blood poisoning or sepsis was another close call.

Whenever the school called the office, my body braced for the punch.

"Billy slipped on the cement curb at the bus stop. His head will need stitches."

Did every working mother have these kinds of calls at work? It was daunting. The one causing me the most heartburn was when he went missing at age seven. He had called me from school to ask if he could stay later to watch a soccer game. By five o'clock he still wasn't home. Panicking, I called the school, but they couldn't find him anywhere. I called the police and described what he was wearing, and they sent out an alarm to look for him. I was frantic. The minutes slowly ticked by, adding to my growing agitation. Wringing my hands, I tried every form of deep-breathing therapy. Minutes turned to hours as I kept checking in with the police. Fidgeting with nerves, I went out on my porch to get some air, silently praying with closed eyes, when I heard his small voice.

"Hi Mom. I missed my bus and walked home." That would have been five long miles—with his short little legs. By taking a shortcut through the park, he apparently was under the radar of police. I was a wreck.

Although very professional in my duties by day, I was determined to make our family time together the centerpiece of our life. Weekends became a marathon of shopping, cooking, baking, and freezing so that dinnertime could still be a sacred event. My food editor background would not allow a simple meatloaf. I challenged myself towards as many creative stews as my Crock-Pot could handle. Stitching together a family life and a professional life was rewarding in many ways, but dinnertime was the high point.

Over my years working closely with food professionals, I internalized how sacred mealtime can and should be. For chefs, cooking is a meaningful expression of who you are. For them the food they served reflected something of them, their land and their soul, in order to create a bonding and memorable experience. Continuously curious about new food trends, I began a project to interview emerging news chefs moving Chicago into more sophisticated culinary experiences. I wanted to know specifically about the ingredients they were using to create their imprimatur. It was the late eighties. Charlie Trotter with his new restaurant Charlie Trotter's, had turned Chicago from a steak-and-potatoes kind of town into a culinary capital. What were his tricks? I had to know. One day, sitting with him in his restaurant kitchen, Charlie Trotter constructed his thinking for me "The leftover edible nasturtiums from our floral display can be used to infuse vinegar with new flavor. That peppery flavor will enhance salads or my next fish dish," he said. I was enthralled. I put Charlie together with the New York culinary star John Georges Vongerichten to present and discuss their brilliantly infused vinegars and oils to a Chicago professional food society. After that meeting Jean Georges invited me to a late dinner with his chef friend Gabino Sotelino of the famed Chicago restaurant Ambria. When we arrived at 10 pm Chef Sotelino brought a bottle of Dom Perignon to the table and said, "What can I cook for you my friend?" The meal ended at midnight and I was enthralled to witness how chefs cook for each other and share ideas. It was an inciteful food experience.

Both my professional life and my family life were now in balance bringing me a solid feeling of contentment. By now I had internalized that life will take unpredictable turns and detours.

Retiring from my professional life, I turned to art as my next creative outlet. Laying out oil paints on my palate, ready to be mixed, I often think about how similar painting is to the real canvas of life. Lives are colorful, layered with good choices, bad calls, indiscretion, lies, luck, mistakes, sadness, dysfunction, ineptitude, regret, surprises, successes, and joys with bright notes and sad notes, all mixed together. At the end of the day, after painting, I mix my unused oil paints on my palate and make beautiful swirls of, guess what, gray. That is what you get with a fully explored life, when the joys and dangers and regrets are all mixed together. Gray is the intermediate between black and white, and it can be beautiful. As I have aged, I am at ease with gray. It is my comfort zone.

One day I noticed subconscious emotions emerging in my art. At first hidden from my own awareness, my drawings revealed a recurring theme. Mother-and-child sketches were stacking up. What was I searching for?.

Soon there were plenty of grandchildren enriching my life. Our family was expanding as Bill's older children added many more dimensions to our lives, especially with each and every new grandchild. As the grandchildren grew they tackled challenging careers in medicine and the media, sharing stories of their adventures along the way. Many cakes and candles and celebrations brought us together over the years with the growing clan. When Billy's daughters were born, we were at the hospital to welcome them into the world. I was honored to share that beautiful experience without the heavy sadness surrounding Ann's birth. Those feelings were never erased. They were suppressed, but not forgotten.

Over our many married years Bill and I shared an unusual closeness that I think began with a deep empathy for each other about our early-life challenges. I am sure that helped us also carve a close working relationship, a deep love and an unusual comfort level. Bill often says, "I just like being with you," and that sums it up well.

I was in that beautiful tranquil place when life delivered the next jolt, a letter in my mailbox with someone saying "I think you might be my grandmother."

Epilogue

———~~~———

Stunned by the letter in my hands, I no longer heard the birds, tractors, and other familiar sounds of summer that tranquil summer morning in the vineyard. Hyped with anxiety, I drove the car erratically toward the house, almost veering off the road into the vines. Stooping to retrieve the letter, I slowly digested more details and read on: "My mother has wondered often about her origins: her birth parents, the life they have led, the sort of people they are." The letter went on, "My mother was born on December 1, 1962, in a suburb of Philadelphia. She was adopted by my grandparents, two of the kindest and most loving people."

My emotions were jumbled and confused, thinking about the conflict of remembered pain and the promise of closure. I rested my head on the back seat to catch my breath. Closing my eyes, I thought back to that cold December day and my ride down the long ramp to deliver Ann to strangers. Shivering with these memories, I knew this letter was reopening wounds buried so long ago. But it was also exciting to think of finally learning what happened after that sorrowful moment that was so deeply etched in my soul.

Walking into our house, I shouted frantically for Bill, but he was nowhere inside.

Scanning the vineyard, I saw his silhouette between the rows, bent over the vines, shears in hand and a roll of green tape flowing down from his belt. He was relaxing in his own silent retreat with an activity he calls "the Zen of pruning and tying vines." Growing up in an orphan home, this pastoral setting is the contrast he always sought. It brings him peace. After eighty-some turbulent years in the fast-paced world, he took Voltaire's advice to "tend your own garden." Carefully cutting away the

old growth on the vines and laying down the new shoots to be tied, this practice is like yoga, so completely soothing.

Breaking the spell of this relaxing moment, I ran up to him and began reading the letter with my voice cracking, the paper rattling, and tears streaming down my checks.

He stopped pruning to observe my frenzied state and asked me to read it again.

It went on. "My Mother has led a full and happy life, so if you would not like to pursue further contact, you can rest assured that your daughter has grown up to be an incredible human being."

Now my heart was thumping.

"If you would like to write back, however, my sister and I would be thrilled and delighted to hear from you." The words were slowly sinking into my new reality. I had often wondered where she was, what she was like, what she would be doing at various points of her life, and now the answers were in reach. Bill listened as I read and wondered aloud if it might be some form of blackmail.

That carefully crafted handwritten letter had taken weeks to write and days to arrive at my rural box.

Running back to the house, it took me only seconds to text a message to Billy: "The letter that I thought might come one day arrived!" He knew what I meant.

Billy was ensconced in a meeting at a tech startup where multitasking was the work style. This would catch his attention. It did.

He called immediately to ask, "Mom, what did it say? After listening to me talk he said, "Are you OK? I can't tell. How are you feeling about this?"

Then, the tears flowed, and I choked out, "Wow, I wasn't expecting this. It's a shock, a bit disorienting ... but I want to follow up."

Explaining his dad's reservation about the authenticity of the letter, Billy said he would look into it. "I'll sort it out, Mom. Give me a few minutes."

He dropped what he was doing to start a search. Within minutes he found an important detail—my daughter's maiden name. This name was very familiar to me. It was the same last name as Marion and her husband. That sealed for me that this was indeed my daughter and two granddaughters reaching out to me after fifty-two years. Did Marion adopt her?

"I am twenty-two years old," the hand-written note went on, "living in Austin at the moment. My mother has led a full and happy life, so if you would not like to pursue further contact, you can rest assured that your daughter has grown to be an incredible human being." That took my breath away.

> My mother, Ann, was born on December 1st, 1962 in the suburbs of Philadelphia. She was adopted by my grandparents, who are two of the kindest and most loving people I know. My mother has wondered often about her origins: her birth parents, the life they have led, the sort of people they are. My sister and I have wondered as well, and a few years ago began exploring the Internet to see what we could discover with what little we had to go on. It is that search that led us to believe that you may be my mother's biological mother, my grandmother. If we are wrong about this, then I apologize for

What would I respond? I immediately starting to formulate a letter in my mind. I wondered what I could possibly say that would adequately explain a lifetime of shame from a pregnancy of rape to my own granddaughter. They hadn't lived through the restrictive era I had, the isolation and humiliation for both me and my family. It was all floating through my mind ... but I wanted to start off on a more positive note.

Without an email address, I had to reply in longhand and send it through snail mail.

"How exciting to hear that you may be my granddaughter," I wrote. "That was such a sweet letter, and I am excited to know you. There is much to explore from my painful journey beginning with an incident my senior year in college. I will be thrilled to take you through the chapters of my life. Thank you for initiating this odyssey. Mine was a rough ride but looking forward to unfolding it with you."

A quick email reply followed from my twenty-three-year-old granddaughter. It began, "First of all, I must say that I was fairly ecstatic when I found your letter in my mailbox and ran back to my apartment like a madwoman, letter in hand, nearly losing my mail key in the process. Just want you to know that I feel overtaken by how eloquent and surreal and gorgeous your letter is. I put my sister and mother on the phone and read and re-read your letter to them until they were thoroughly satisfied, saying it is better than I thought it could be. I am so very happy to hear back from you and that you are so gracious and interested in sharing with us. This will be a special experience, indeed, and am excited to be here at the beginning."

Ann wrote, "The girls and I are so excited about the chance of meeting. I am still in shock of all that has transpired over the last few weeks. I woke up thinking about you. I have a busy day giving a four-hour lecture on brain injury/cognitive impairment and behavior." I learned Ann is a professor working towards a Ph.D. I am so thrilled and proud of her already.

And now, I had to do the hard work of reaching back into my secret life and relive each of the disturbing chapters. I had to organize my thoughts and put them on paper. It was just what Miriam had always wanted me to do, to finally tell my story.

One dilemma was what to tell Billy's young daughters, who were five and eight. At bedtime, I would crawl under the covers with them while putting them to bed and say, "Let's tell stories."

"You go first, grandma," they would say. Although they had mounds of books, they preferred my stories, mostly about Billy and his friends.

Telling tales gave them a richer image of their dad's life growing up in a household as an only child. My stories detailed our center-entrance Colonial by a beach where he sold lemonade to befriend the lifeguards, and his room and the clothes chute he tried to crawl through to the other bedroom, and his friends who gathered at our house for mischief and to watch the Chicago Bulls games They pleaded for more stories about his life until we fell asleep.

What would I tell them now? How would I begin to explain "Your Daddy has a sister he never knew." That would require a long explanation with a delicate touch. They were too young, too impressionable, to understand the nuances of rape and the taboos surrounding unwed mothers and illegitimacy from so long ago. Yet I knew that one day they would need to know the whole story. And, so with many days of tears streaming down my cheeks, I began unraveling my story and reliving all the painful details of times when society dictated our destiny.

For my daughter Ann, for her daughters, and for Billy's daughters, the telling was about to begin. I would start by sharing the positives in my life with them, and then work back to that night on a college campus that turned my life upside down. It was going to be a turbulent ride, but I was finally ready.

A flurry of emails followed that first letter in my rural mailbox. I wrote, "This is like a fairy tale for me, waking up to find a daughter and two granddaughters."

As I wrote fragments of my life for Ann and her daughters, they were sealed with the hope that they would understand the underlying reasons for adoption. Those were very different times marked by a finger-wagging public.

The process of writing and revisiting my early calamity was cathartic. Recalling details unleashed so many emotions that tears started to blotch my keyboard. It was like lancing a boil, especially when remembering my long ride down the hospital ramp on a cold dark December day fifty-two years before. My emotions as I wrote were just as raw.

Ann responded: "Your Chicago years were fascinating, and how gutsy you were! I love learning about you this way. It will be a great story for my girls of how life was and how courage moved you forward."

She went on, "I was overcome with emotion, reading your email after work last night. I was awake late wondering how to relay to you about myself and my life. I am full of excitement with so many stories to share. It is mind-boggling."

She added, "I know there is pain from your ordeal in 1962, but I have told the girls we will discuss it when we see you in person. I felt very connected to you when I had my first daughter because I could not imagine letting her go. I was thrilled when she had my eyes … finally someone who looked like me! I cried a lot during the movie *Philomena*. It was my daughter's idea to see it, and she sobbed the whole way through it. I thought about you and the life you must have had!"

I could feel the healing beginning to take hold. I relaxed into the rhythm of our exchanges.

Pictures of Ann's daughters showed they resembled Pete. Were they curious about him as well? Had they ever met him?

Ann answered that she had pieced together parts of my story from Marion and knew I had gone to Penn State. Knowing Pete's name from the birth certificate, they easily found him in the Penn State yearbook. Leafing through the pages from 1962, his picture was in plain sight. I wondered how Ann felt, staring at her father for the first time.

They found me in the yearbook as well, but under my maiden name. Without a clue to my married name, the trail went cold. There were no clues anywhere. Then, just a few months before, new clues emerged to where this mystery mother might be. Looking online, they found my maiden name linked to an art show in California. Professionally, I had taken my maiden name as a middle name and used it again in my artist's profile. Bingo! With a little help from technology, she was able to pinpoint my address.

All our stars were lined up when that letter arrived in my mailbox that summer morning.

At various stages of my life, I would stop and count how old Ann might be. When Bill's four children came into my life, Ann would have been around eight, a delicate age for any surprises. As Billy was growing up, I thought my story of rape and pregnancy was inappropriate for him to hear quite yet. Over the years I would think, "Somewhere out there I have a daughter, ten years older than Billy." But I always felt it was best to let her own parents have their role without complications. I didn't try to find her. It had been their privilege and role to raise her. But I remember thinking of her in her twenties, then her thirties. I never lost track.

Billy, too, had been writing to Ann and the girls, "Hi everyone. It has been so exciting reading your stories and getting to know you all, I thought I would chime in with a little about me, my wife, and two daughters." I was proud of him for entering in without reservation.

At some point, I will fill Ann in on my own stroke, but that is yet to come. Imagine—I have a daughter who is a nurse practitioner and teaching professor at a leading East Coast university.

Pictures of her revealed a happy childhood. I felt a huge sense of relief. Then we noticed an interesting similarity. We had both spent many summers sailing. While Bill, Billy, and I were sailing Lake Michigan and the Great Lakes, Ann was sailing with her dad in Chesapeake Bay and even from Bermuda to Maine. We shared the thrill of sailing.

Leading up to our much-anticipated first meeting, my mind was fluttering in anticipation. Would she hold any resentments or just open her arms to me? Such serendipity. Soon, I would be able to look deep into the eyes of my lost daughter.

Ann and her girls were coming to San Francisco to meet me, but Ann and I had wanted to meet privately first. By the same fireplace where I emotionally told Billy about Ann, I would sit facing her for the first time, in my apartment, without the clatter of restaurant noises or distracting visuals. I envisioned that moment right down to the details of what food to serve.

The evening she was about to arrive, the anticipation of the moment was building. I flitted through the apartment arranging pillows and ended in the kitchen to once again check on my squash-and-pear soup on the stove. My homegrown roasted French butter pears added a sweetness to the simmering delicata squash. I nervously fumbled to finish baking off Parmesan croutons. Then I glanced at the at clock; she was due any moment. I took a deep breath and opened the Sauvignon Blanc. My doggedly punctual self always had dinners organized well ahead of time. I was more than ready for this moment, a fifty-two-year reunion.

It would be our own quiet moment together, mother and child, looking into each other's eyes, seeking similarities and commonalities. Who would I see when I opened the door? Would she have any of my gestures, my physical moves? Would I have that immediate sense of kinship? There were so many chapters of time and space between us. The suspense was building.

We'd both fantasized how this moment would play out. On her flight in that evening she wrote in a note, "As I look at the Philly skyline fade away, I head to a town I know. I don't know, though, how anxiety, excitement, curiosity, wonder, and mystery are about to be resolved. I feel like I am in slow motion, my life in review. Am I this mother's child? How will we know if a bond still exists? Is it a word, a touch, or just a lot of tears?"

Author Notes

The reunion was an awesome moment of tears and pure joy as we flung our arms around each other and stepped back to take a good look at who each had become. Ann had the familiar smile of my family but the dark hair and taller stature of her father—a definite blend. It warmed my whole being to hear about her happy early life. It was exactly what I had always hoped she'd had. That first meeting was a long-awaited closure, a mix of curiosity satisfied with reassurance. We reminisced about the parts we knew and wondered aloud, each with questions the other offered to answer. Over candlelight and wine, the evening flew by, filled with shared stories filling in the unknowns. The missing chapters of our lives were finally being revealed.

We could hardly eat with the excitement and questions each had for the other. Ann explained what she knew about her first days with her parents. Dr. Andy had approached her mother in the fall of 1962 and wondered if she would like to adopt a baby. Marion's husband and Ann's father were brothers, and that is how I recognized her maiden name. Her dad was an airline pilot who was often away, so when he came home from a trip one day, her mother asked, "What if we add another to the family?" They already had one daughter and were concerned if I could really be able to give up a child. They opted to keep it a secret that a baby might be coming into the household.

Ann told me, "Moving into their new house December third, they were thinking you weren't delivering until Christmas. Your early delivery was a shock. When they got the call you were heading into labor at Thanksgiving, my mom in a panic had to borrow some baby clothes. The move into the new house was stressful enough. Two of the town's baby nurses, Miss Iona and Miss Olivia, came to the hospital and picked me up from you on that hospital ramp. It was a very cold and icy day, and the moving van slid down the street into a ditch. Apparently the nurses brought me back to my mom, who wrapped me inside her jacket while they completed the move."

Laughing through the stories and details we shared that night was a question Ann had for me. She said she had always wondered, "Did you remember my birthday each year?" Although she had a blissful childhood, she never stopped wondering about me and our connection.

I was not sure how to honestly answer her about the birthdays. Sometimes I did, but my survival technique through the years was to push down any memories surrounding her birth. She, as most adoptive children, was trying to cling to the few pieces and details she knew. I never realized how adoption does not always give a child the closure they need, but when is the right time for details? At what age?

Certainly, we were now getting into it with some intriguing answers to long-unanswered questions. It was bonding and beautiful. She was a lovely surprise for me in my later years, the daughter I lost, and the mother she had found. She could see that I had been a survivor, never giving in, fighting for a life I could control rather than be victimized. I could see that she had some of my drive working on her Ph.D. in her fifties. I was enormously proud she had chosen to help people through her chosen profession as nurse practitioner.

That night, as promised, I recounted for her details of "the incident" that night that had haunted me the rest of my life. I could tell in her eyes that she felt my pain. She was reliving my anguish as I was letting go of it. I sensed I was forgiven and respected for my journey and my decisions at that very moment.

The next day Billy and his wife were bringing their girls to meet Ann and her daughters. They were told they were going to meet some cousins they didn't yet know. Holding my breath, I hoped they would not be too inquisitive. It wasn't the right time for reality.

This amazing reunion took place at a restaurant overlooking the San Francisco Bay with the silhouette of sailboats off in the distance. Over bowls of steamed mussels and toasted warm sourdough, we dipped bread in the broth and shared our own sailing stories of distant waters and so much more. It was surreal. I glanced out to sea while listening to their talk. Here were my two natural children meeting for the first time and sharing sailing stories dear to them. Ann's daughters joined in while the youngest granddaughters sat there without a clue as to their real relationship.

The next day, Billy's young daughters were asked what they did on the weekend. "We got dressed up in our fancy dresses and went to lunch with cousins. Then we played on the rocks outside. It was so much fun." I knew then I would need to tell my story in a way they could understand some day about a tragic incident, the very different times, their daddy's sister lost to adoption, my rough journey forward, and the difficult decisions Grandma had to make along the way so many years ago.

A Letter to My Granddaughters

To my dear granddaughters,

Learn from my journey. My self-esteem, ambition, certainty, and reputation were instantly erased and replaced with stigma. Raped and pregnant, my dignity had been stolen. I was desperate to get it back. Feel the shame and the pain in my story that I and so many other women had to endure.

Moralists and harsh laws held us in their grip. As an unmarried pregnant woman, no mind the rape part, it was a time when society scolded you. They rejected sex for single women. Forced marriages were common, while others had the fearsome task of taking an unwanted pregnancy to term. Think about how it might feel to nurture a baby in your body for nine months only to hand it over to strangers. That act of severance was a heavy price to pay. As a college student the challenges seemed bigger than me. I knew children of the unmarried were labeled "bastards," and the women who bore them as "tramps." The shame was implicit. Digging back into my story from over fifty years ago, I deconstructed it with fresh insights to share. Hopefully, if life ever delivers you a punch that kicks you in the gut, you can learn from the next few pages what most sustained me, nurtured me and centered me to keep fighting for my dignity. I had to jump hurdles to get out of my dilemma, but my family had given me the foundation to do so. That plus a bit of grit and loads of determination.

Today it is not uncommon for a single woman to bear a child. There are more liberal attitudes now towards sexuality and the use of birth control. But, in my day the humiliation hung over me like a dark, heavy cloak as if the rape and the resulting pregnancy were my fault.

Writing *The Unravelling* was hard. It brought back wrenching memories and a flood of tears, but the very act of writing them down brought the fresh air of acceptance and the additional gift of clarity. I could finally understand how the pieces of my assault that night so many years ago fit together.

Not my fault. Rape and shame were synonymous. One of the most important revelations came to me only recently that what happened to me was not my fault. For years I had felt shame about the rape and kept it buried as a deep dark secret. What I did not realize then was that the shame I was feeling should not have been mine, but the perpetrator's. He was the aggressor who shuffled me to the upstairs of his fraternity, where no women were allowed, just for his pleasure. I was the victim. I was the one violated, and I had to endure the pain of isolation and the trauma of childbirth. I was sentenced to deliver a baby with indelible scars from the experience. My future had slowly turned into a tragedy while he simply walked away.

Shame is a potent form of control. The finger of shame has historically been wagged at women. In my day I just expected it. A Plymouth law back in1694 had women sewing the letter A for adultery in their clothes for the public to see. Nathaniel Hawthorne reflected on these times with his book *The Scarlet Letter*. The letter A heaped shame on women for having sex outside marriage. I knew from literature that in each generation the male character involved was free and unencumbered.

If it is not consent, it's rape. Date rape and acquaintance rape were terms never used in my day. Rape at knifepoint was understandably rape. We weren't expecting someone we knew would sense our vulnerability and move in for the kill. That feeling of degradation sinks you. At the time I did not know the definition of rape. Maybe it has been adjusted over the years, but one of its definitions is taking advantage of someone drugged or drunk. Consent makes it an even playing field. I had been raped. It wasn't my fault.

Trauma clouds your recall. Since I could never recall exactly what happened, only fragments, it became a hard story to tell, so I didn't. How could I share a story when the details were scrambled? With my inability to piece it together, I felt humiliated but recently learned that the fragments were actually quite normal. Apparently, the brain encodes traumatic experiences as fragments, often as flashbacks. It was disturbing to me then that I could not explain the events of that night. The context and sequence of events were mixed up. The bits and pieces were just not meshing together. But, learning that traumatic experiences impact the brain, I finally could understand why my memory had been so fuzzy.

Forced marriage is not a solution. Where did I get the emotional mettle to reject the idea of marriage as a solution to unwanted pregnancy? That was my first act of courage. I quickly summed up just how it would feel to marry someone who had such little respect for me. While women from my era did marry under similar circumstances, some ended up in psychoanalysis. I never allowed my feelings of humiliation to turn into feelings of denigration, or worse, spread darkly into depression. I knew I had gone through a devastating experience but needed to work my way out of it. It felt like

I was in a box, but I owned it and didn't have time for self-pity. Instead of wallowing in regret, I strengthened my resolve and was desperate to get back into society's fold.

Sexual assault betrays trust and affection. The rape had stolen my sense of trust. I became very cautious about men and kept my protective armor in place. My sexual spontaneity was always in check. Had I been able to tell my story then I would have discovered there were so many sisters also suffering in silence. The "Me Too Movement" has opened a floodgate of stories of coercive bosses in the workplace and an alarming number of campus assaults. When the powerful have control over you, you feel helpless. That was the story of my generation. Hopefully, your generation will be talking.

Storytelling relieves pain. It took me way too long to tell my story, first in the comfort of your grandpa's arms, then tearfully to my longtime friend, and finally to your dad when he was college aged. Each telling brought up waves of pent-up emotion. Getting outside of your comfort zone to reach into pain will have its rewards. Never underestimate the support your friends can be. My sorority sisters, when finally told years later at one of our many reunions, offered, "Why couldn't you tell us? We would have understood." To my surprise, I found that with each and every telling, healing took place. When I sent a sketch of my story to my oldest friend Georgia, she instantly called and her first words were "You are not alone. It happened to me." After all those lunches we had together in our twenties, we never shared our deepest secrets.

Coping skills. I knew I could cope. I was adaptive. No one would know from the self-assured, well-dressed, attractive image I projected in my twenties that inside some part of me suffered in silence. I rose to heights in the business world few women of the day would experience. With each career advancement, I propelled myself into new roles and new challenges. My confidence grew because my parents had given me a firm foundation of love and support in my early years. Maybe simply because my dad taught me to own up to a lie as a very young child, I learned to embrace and own what happens to me. I am so grateful to them for fostering in me strong feelings of security within myself. My healthy thinking that "I can get through this" was well integrated.

A nurturing family helps. My mom had a way of wrapping us up in her love, her cocoon, through food. The cooking aromas drifting through our house were locked in my memories during my rough times. Dense chocolate baking on cold winter nights would tease us into her kitchen. If it wasn't her rich chocolate sauce bubbling up on the stove, it was the fragrance of a sumptuous chocolate cake baking in the oven. To this day, if I am feeling down or out of sorts, I head to my kitchen to bake something chocolate. I seek out the best chocolate I can buy. In fact, I have stockpiled my kitchen with an eleven pound block of Belgian Bittersweet Chocolate. I also use imported cocoa like French Barry cocoa powder or Pernigotti Dutch cocoa. When company is coming, I often throw together a batch of triple chocolate biscotti just to fill the air with that sensuous scent of chocolate. It makes my house feel like the home I knew, filled with chocolaty aromas and love.

When life throws you a curve bake my biscotti, or do whatever else centers you to keep you grounded. Maybe write down your own stories or paint the sunset but baking comforts me the most.

My Triple Chocolate Biscotti

2 cups flour
1/2 cup good quality Dutch process cocoa
1 1/2 teaspoons baking powder
1/2 teaspoon baking soda
1/2 teaspoon salt
1 stick (4 ounces) unsalted butter
1 cup of granulated sugar
2 eggs
1 teaspoon vanilla
1/2 cup chocolate-covered espresso beans
1/2 cup bite-size chunks of bittersweet chocolate or chocolate chips
1 cup of very coarsely chopped walnuts

Mix the dry ingredients together: flour, cocoa, baking powder, baking soda, and salt.

With a paddle beater, whip the butter and sugar together until creamy and light. Add eggs one at a time and continue beating. Add the vanilla.

Add all the dry ingredients and mix until blended. Then, add the walnuts, chocolate chunks, and chocolate-covered espresso beans.

Divide the dough in half. On a baking sheet, make two logs of the dough, and smooth it with a knife to approximately 3 inches by 10 inches.

Bake at 325 degrees for 30 minutes. Remove from oven and cool ten minutes. Slice cookie bars on the diagonal and turn on their side. Return to oven for 15 more minutes.

Biscotti are always twice baked, and the aromas fill the kitchen twice, too.

About the Author

Meredith's writing skills, honed with a career as food editor of a leading restaurant magazine, copy writer for top advertising agencies, publicist and marketing executive, helped her articulate trauma and the emotional topography of rape plus the blistering consequences she endured. She poignantly puts a spotlight on the times when social mores drove thousands of women into hiding then suffer the human pain of severance of mother and child. Art has also given her depth of expression as her drawings related back to her early personal trauma. Today she finds solace growing grapes in Northern California, painting the ever changing drama in wine country and writing.

Meredith's art practice later in life led her to draw images of women and sometimes women in remorse. She was drawn to the compelling emotion of August Rodin's Eve, After the Fall, a sculpture housed in the Legion of Honor Museum in San Francisco. "Without even knowing the title of the work, I sat down to draw it impulsively right there in the museum one day. It spoke to me. I know it speaks to many women who have suffered a sexual assault and suffer in silence." It is the image she chose for the cover.

For All Women to Know

Mine was a journey for younger women to contemplate and for older women to remember. That shadowy period when pregnant women had no control over their bodies should never be forgotten. We paid a price for our silence. There is a sisterhood of women with similar experiences to my own and their own hidden secrets. Our scars will never go away. The blemishes are there as a reminder of the hurdles that we and our families had to endure. Our stories need to be heard and understood from the perspective of those dark times before Roe v. Wade made abortion a legal option, when women were forced to carry a child to term. History can repeat itself with women again facing unwanted pregnancy without control over their destiny. For those who find themselves unintentionally pregnant, it may not be a celebratory time: not for those graduating with serious college debt, a new issue for the times, not for victims of rape or incest, not for battered and abused women, or for those who just earned a much-needed scholarship. It is definitely not good news for those heading even deeper into poverty.

Looking back, as an inexperienced young woman, I had many hard decisions to make. Late in life, the sweetest part of my bittersweet story was meeting my daughter Ann and her daughters. Our sweet reunion brought me joy and the ultimate closure to a pain that had lasted fifty-two years. I am so proud to know she devoted her life helping others in the medical profession as a Ph.D. nurse practitioner. She, too, had grit.

My art practice later in life had led me to draw images of women in remorse. I was drawn to the compelling emotion of Auguste Rodin's *Eve, After the Fall*, housed in the Legion of Honor Museum in San Francisco. Without even knowing the title of the work, I sat down to draw it impulsively there in the museum one day. It spoke to me. I know it speaks to many women. It is the image on this book cover. At the same time mother and child images were stacking up in my studio as well. Painting and drawing the human figure became my passion, and apparently it was part of my healing process.

Additional Suggested Readings

Collins, Gail. *When Everything Changed - The Amazing Journey of American Women from 1960 to Present.* Little, Brown and Company, 2009

Fessler, Ann. *The Girls Who Went Away - The Hidden History of Women Who Surrendered Children for Adoption in the Decades Before Roe v. Wade.* Penguin Books, 2006

Glaser, Gabrielle. *American Baby - A Mother, A Child and The Shadow History of Adoption,* Penguin Random House LLC, 2021

Krakauer, Jon. *Missoula - Rape and the Justice System in a College Town.* Barnes and Noble, 2015

Miller, Chanel. *Know My Name - Including Her strong Victim Impact Statement at a Sentencing Hearing.* Viking, 2019

Minister, Meredith. *Rape Culture on Campus. Lexington Press, 2018.*

Parker, Dr. Willie. *Life's Work - A Moral Argument for Choice.* Atria Books, 2017

Reagan, Leslie. *When Abortion Was a Crime - Women, Medicine and Law In the United States, 1867-1973.* University of California Press, September, 1998.

Richards, Cecile. *Make Trouble - To Make Change You Have to Make Trouble.*

San Filippo, Christina. *Why Women Should Make The Abortion Decision: Damned if you Do and Damned if you Don't.* Ramapo College, New Jersey, September, 2020

Schwartz, Dr. Arielle. *The Neurobiology of Traumatic Memory - Why Survivors Forget.* Blog posted October 12, 2018 by Arielle Schwartz.

Touchstone, 2018

Wilson-Buterbaugh, Karen. *The Baby Scoop Era - Unwed Mothers, Infant adoption and Forced Surrender.* Karen Wilson-Buterbaugh, 2019.